—The Power of Holy Habits—

WILLIAM H. HINSON

THE POWER OF HOLY HABITS

A Discipline for Faithful Discipleship

ABINGDON PRESS / NASHVILLE

THE POWER OF HOLY HABITS

Copyright © 1991 by Abingdon Press

This book is printed on recycled, acid-free paper.

Library of Congress Cataloging-in-Publication Data

Hinson, William H., 1936–
 The power of holy habits: a discipline for faithful discipleship
/William H. Hinson.
  p. cm.
 ISBN 0-687-33200-1 (alk. paper)
 1. Christian life—Methodist authors. 2. Church membership.
I. Title.
BV4501.2.H5215   1990
248.4'876—dc20

91-7894
CIP

Scripture quotations, except where specifically noted, are from the New Revised Standard Version of the Bible, copyright © 1990 by the Division of Christian Education, National Council of Churches of Christ in the U.S.A. Used by permission.

Scripture quotations marked NIV are taken from the *Holy Bible: New International Version.* Copyright © 1973, 1978, 1984 by the International Bible Society. Used by permission of Zondervan Bible Publishers.

Scripture quotations marked NJB are from *The New Jerusalem Bible,* copyright © 1985 by Darton, Longman, and Todd, and Doubleday & Company, Inc. Reprinted by permission of the publishers.

Scripture quotations marked "Williams" are from *The New Testament in Plain English* by Charles Kingsley Williams, copyright © 1963 by Charles Kingsley Williams.

MANUFACTURED IN THE UNITED STATES OF AMERICA

—— To ——

**Montene and J. P. Morris,
Donnie, Mickey, and Kathy**

_The love of the Morris family has from our earliest years been a
source of strength and encouragement and remains so until this
day._

FOREWORD

This book is a blending of inspiration, instruction, and practical advice for those who have recently joined the church and for those who wish to renew their commitment to Christ and to the church.

New members are not particularly interested in studying the structure of our connectional church, and they are not very eager to plunge into a theological study of the church. They are, however, grateful for any practical help in keeping their membership vows, and for assistance in making good on all of the promises implied in joining the church.

I have observed that those persons who join our church and attend our new-member class become more involved and active in the total ministry of the church. They pledge to the budget, teach Sunday school, attend church, and serve in a multitude of ways. My staff and I believe the curriculum in those orientation classes plays an important part in making members into disciples. The ten chapters in this little book contain the essence of what we say to our new and not-so-new members who want to be genuine disciples.

This book has been written and printed with the hope that it can be placed in the hands of those who are beginning—or beginning again—their Christian pilgrimage.

I am deeply grateful to Mrs. Elizabeth Finger, my competent and patient secretary. She has not only typed and retyped this manuscript but also has rendered inestimable assistance through her helpful and constructive suggestions.

As always, I am indebted to my wife, Jean, whose love and support allow and encourage me to make a faithful response to the call of Christ.

―――――――――

CONTENTS

1

—— PRAYER ——

Inward Communion

He went up the mountain and called to him those whom he wanted, and they came to him. And he appointed twelve, whom he also named apostles, to be with him, and to be sent out to proclaim the message, and to have authority to cast out demons. So he appointed the twelve: Simon (to whom he gave the name Peter); James son of Zebedee and John the brother of James (to whom he gave the name Boanerges, that is, Sons of Thunder); and Andrew, and Philip, and Bartholomew, and Matthew, and Thomas, and James son of Alphaeus, and Thaddaeus, and Simon the Cananaean, and Judas Iscariot, who betrayed him. (Mark 3:13-19)

During the summer of 1988, I heard Dr. Noah Langdale, president of Georgia State University, address a class of graduating seniors. In that address, he told them that every century has its outstanding fact. For instance, he said that the outstanding fact in England during the eighteenth century was its navy. As I was leaving the coliseum following the graduation ceremonies, I heard a small group of people challenging Dr. Langdale's comment concerning the British navy. They had their own theories about what was most important. As I continued out of the coliseum, I concluded that I also had a

11

different understanding. As one of almost sixty million people on the earth who are called Methodist, I believe that the most important fact of early eighteenth-century England was that Susanna Wesley was teaching her children—in the parsonage at Epworth, England—to be persons of prayer.

When the story of our own Christian commitment is written, if we have been faithful and effective disciples, the salient fact in that faithfulness will be traced to a life of prayer. What is true about modern disciples has always been true of the followers of Jesus, including the original apostles.

We don't know a great deal about the twelve disciples. We have miniature character portraits of a few of them. We know something about Peter, James, and John; we know about Thomas; we certainly know about Judas. We know a little bit about several of them, but there is not much hard data on any of them. We had a rash of apocryphal writings at one time in the Church concerning the original twelve, but the writings were just that—apocryphal. It may or may not have happened. We know that their contemporaries called them common, uneducated men. We know that Jesus, true to his character, spent all night in prayer before calling and appointing them to be disciples. He named twelve disciples, obviously reconstituting Israel. Old Israel had twelve tribes; the new Israel would have twelve apostles. We know that Jesus authorized the disciples to preach and to heal. We have spent a great deal of thought and effort in trying to come to terms with the implications of a preaching, healing ministry.

The first duty of a disciple is the least talked about, but the most important one of all—to be with Jesus. Our Lord appointed his disciples and ordained them to be with him. To be with Jesus is our first responsibility as followers.

John Wesley called prayer the first means of grace. He

said that it is a grand means of drawing near to God. A lack of prayer, on the other hand, is primarily responsible for what Wesley referred to as "the wilderness state," that is, spiritual dryness and purposelessness.

Our forebears apparently agreed with both Jesus and Mr. Wesley about the importance of prayer. Our initial promise to support the church is a well-placed one in that we promise to support the church "with our prayers." We can rightly assume that anyone who takes that initial vow seriously and prays for the church will also be responsive to all of the other vows one has taken. Praying Christians will gladly worship, give, and serve in those ministries that they support with their prayers.

That prayer must be a holy habit for the Christian cannot be denied. In the eighteenth chapter of Luke, Jesus declares that we ought to pray "always and not to lose heart" (vs. 1).

In the next chapter, when we discuss our promise to support the church with our presence, we will examine the interesting phrase "as was his custom," which appears only twice in the Gospels. We will see that it appears first when describing Jesus' pattern of worship on the Sabbath. The phrase appears a second time when describing Jesus going to the Garden of Gethsemane, which was his place of prayer. Jesus went to prayer "as was his custom" when he was in Jerusalem. Jesus had times and places for prayer. Prayer for him was specific, intentional, and a part of who he was.

When I was a student at Boston University, I was given an assignment by Dr. Howard Thurman to write a fifty-five page paper on the prayer life of Jesus. I was not permitted to use a concordance or any reference book other than the Bible. I struggled with that assignment for days. I virtually lived with Jesus through the Holy Scriptures. Before I concluded the paper, I realized that my own spiritual life had deepened as a result of being with Jesus in the times, places, and kinds of prayers he prayed.

When Dr. Thurman had graded my paper and given it back to me, I was curious as to what he might have written on my paper. There were no red marks, and there was only this sentence at the end of my paper, "I hope you have learned through this experience that one does not pray in order to be religious, but to be true to the grain in one's own wood." Everything that we are, or ever will become, is predicated upon our being with Jesus.

All of us stand in need of the restoration that is possible only through communion with Christ. I was thinking about that restoration not long ago when I was visiting the hospital. I was waiting near the nurses' station to see a patient who was a member of my church. The nurse working behind the desk kept humming an old gospel hymn, but she wouldn't finish it. She kept humming the part of the hymn that reads "tempted and tried." Then she'd work a little bit and hum that same phrase once more—tempted and tried. Finally, after hearing her hum the same phrase four or five times, I whistled the rest of it for her. The startled nurse looked in my direction, nudged her companion, and said, "That man just whistled my song." I said, "Lady, someone needed to finish it." You can't just whistle about being tempted and tried; you must go on and finish it. Say "We need a great Savior." That's where we all come out. Apart from the inspiration and the strength of Christ within us, we get bogged down in our defeats, begin to whine, and complain. We need someone who sets us on our feet and sends us out with renewed vigor and strength.

Our God has not given us a spirit of fear and timidity, but instead offers us love, power, and self-control. We must be very careful that we do not do as Mary and Joseph did on their way back to Nazareth.

In the Gospel of Luke, we are told about the trip to

Jerusalem that Mary and Joseph made with the boy Jesus when our Lord was twelve years of age. At the end of their visit in the Holy City, Mary and Joseph started back to Nazareth, leaving the child Jesus behind. We need not wonder about how loving parents could leave their son behind. It was especially easy for one to be left behind in biblical days. The men and the women often traveled in separate groups. Sometimes a group of men would leave early; the women would leave a bit later, and then the last group of men would bring up the rear. It was easy for Mary to assume that Jesus had stayed behind with Joseph, and Joseph, in like manner, could easily assume that Jesus had gone on with his mother. The Bible says when they at last made camp that night after traveling all day long, they looked at each other and realized that they had just been "assuming that he [Jesus] was in the group of travelers" (Luke 2:44).

One of the most shocking experiences in all of life is to have traveled a long way down life's highway only to come to a long, dark night and realize that you have only been assuming Jesus to be in your company. When the clock strikes midnight, we cannot begin to do what we should have been doing since early morning.

The wise maidens about whom Jesus spoke were not being selfish when they refused to lend their oil to the foolish maidens who were about to be excluded from the presence of the bridegroom. We can lend many things, but we cannot lend spiritual preparation. We can and should pray for each other, but no one can pray your prayers for you. We cannot assume about being in the company of Christ.

I hear many people say that the worst thing in the world is to lose God. I have never believed that. The worst thing in the world is for someone to lose God and not even know it. Tragedy is to go out like Samson and flex muscles that you

15

no longer have as you prepare to meet your enemy, and then realize that the Lord has departed from you. Tragedy is to prepare to meet the bridegroom at the midnight hour only to discover that your lamp doesn't have any oil in it. Christians can never suppose about being in the company of Jesus.

Once a pastor was talking with me about leaving the ministry. He explained that he had lost the joy of serving. He found no satisfaction in pastoral calling, in counseling, in preaching, or any of the other responsibilities of the clergy. We talked for some time, and I referred him to our conference counselor with whom he could talk things out in great length. As we came to the latter part of our conversation, I asked him to share with me about his prayer time. The free-flowing conversation became strained with an awkward silence. We both realized that he did not have a prayer life.

As this minister left my office, I thought about one of the sayings attributed to Dwight L. Moody. Moody said that those of us in spiritual ministry go bankrupt for the same reason people go bankrupt in the world of business—it's too much business on too little capital.

E. Stanley Jones is reported to have told a story about a bishop who loved the limelight. The bishop's life was not complete unless he was always in the spotlight, the center of attention. When at last the bishop came to retirement, not only was he miserable, but he made everyone else who happened to be around him miserable. Commenting on that bishop, E. Stanley Jones said that the man obviously had a lot in the showroom, but not very much at all in the storeroom. Life does have a way of showing us how much we have in the storeroom. If we do not discover this in our early years, the middle or later years will reveal our spiritual reservoir—or lack of it.

I read the other day that if you cannot afford a cellular

phone you can get a fake antenna for nineteen dollars. Over two hundred thousand people have bought fake antennas. We can fake a lot of things, including a car telephone. We cannot, however, fake a life of prayer. When we come to the midnight hour in our lives, either we have oil in our lamps or we do not. No other means of grace can take the place of prayer.

To talk about being with Jesus sounds rather vague and nebulous to the Western mind. Westerners are action oriented. We want to get on with the program. We have a tendency to forget that each time our Lord wanted to send the early Church on one of his errands, he had to interrupt their prayers to send them out. We are more prone to interrupt our work to have prayers. We struggle as Nouwen has suggested to "overcome the enormous obstacle of activism."

What do we mean, "with Jesus"? Obviously, we do not mean what Malcolm Boyd has suggested when he raises the question in his book *Are You Running with Me, Jesus?* The obvious answer to that is no. Morton Kelsey helps us in his book *Encounter with God* by reminding us that almost half of the verses in the New Testament are spiritually perceived. If we do not cultivate the things of the spirit and have the eyes of our hearts open, we have lost half of the New Testament to begin with.

Recently I heard a prominent anthropologist state that the present age is marked by a deep hunger for the spiritual. People are desperate to find something in which they can believe. We cannot satisfy the deepest needs of people by doing *things*, we must first learn to become something by being with Jesus. Every other responsibility given to his disciples was predicated upon the first duty of a disciple—to be with Jesus.

The great mystic Richard Baxter said that we're

17

beginning to be spiritual when we reach the point when we can say to our worldly cares and concerns what Jesus said to his disciples in the Garden of Gethsemane, "Sit here while I pray" (Mark 14:32). When we can set aside the clamoring voices and demands of the world and become deliberate and intentional in our prayer time, our lives and the life of our church will be full of power. God wants to fill us with power.

One Sunday afternoon I flew out of Houston headed to Columbia, South Carolina, for a series of revival services. I had not slept very well on Saturday evening, had preached twice that Sunday, and was eagerly anticipating a much-needed nap on my way to Atlanta where I could change planes for Columbia. Unfortunately, however, it was not to be because a "talker" sat down beside me, and I didn't get to close my eyes. When I arrived in Atlanta, moreover, the plane to South Carolina was late. When at last we were airborne, I knew the schedule would be extremely close. Church members met me at the airport in Columbia and whisked me off to the church. I didn't get to go by the room to wash my face or freshen up in any way. I arrived at the church just in time to preach.

As I preached that night, I sometimes held to the pulpit because I was swaying a little bit from fatigue. A large congregation was in attendance that evening, and at the end of the service the pastor announced that there would be a reception in the fellowship hall for all of the people to come by to greet the visiting preacher. I wedged myself into the door jamb at the fellowship hall and began to greet an almost endless line of people. Near the end of the line, a large man stepped aside and suddenly I was confronted by my youngest daughter.

Cathy was living in Augusta, Georgia, and attending the Medical College of Georgia in nursing training. When she learned that I was going to be preaching in Columbia, she borrowed her boyfriend's old car, which had a torn headliner and a noisy muffler, and drove some distance to be in the sanctuary that night. She had come, nevertheless, because she wanted to be with her daddy, and needed to talk with me about a lot of things.

We left the church and went out to get some coffee and a piece of pie. Afterwards, we went to my hotel room and talked until it was almost time for Cathy to drive back to Augusta where she would attend an early class. A curious thing happened to me that night. I forgot about my fatigue. I was so touched, and still am, that my child wanted to be with her father and would go to such great lengths to be with me that I would have, if necessary, walked to South Carolina. I would have stayed awake not one night, but several, in order to be there for her. I understood more completely what Jesus had in mind when he said, "If you then, who are evil, know how to give good gifts to your children, how much more will your Father in heaven give good things to those who ask him!" (Matt. 7:11).

Remember that your first responsibility as a Christian disciple is to be a person of prayer. Through your life of prayer, your communion with Christ, our Lord, will give you all of those good gifts that you both need and want.

2
— WORSHIP —
The Upward Look

When he came to Nazareth, where he had been
brought up, he went to the synagogue on the sabbath
day, as was his custom. (Luke 4:16a)

L ife does have a way of boiling us down. In the end, if
we have lived a long life, we are reduced to the
essence of who we are.

My Grandmother Hinson was in her nineties when she
died. During her last years, this remarkable woman, who
wore her long white hair in a bun, became increasingly
confused and feeble. Still, when one of her grandchildren,
family, or friends came within arm's length, he or she
received a hug, a pat, and an "I love you." One of her last
requests was for a grandson to help her sit up in her bed
that she might sing a hymn of praise to God.

By the end of her life there wasn't much left of my
grandmother except love—love for God and other people.
My grandmother had the upward look—worship was a
high priority for her throughout her life.

Jesus also kept his life centered on God through
systematic worship. Jesus and the Jews worshiped in a
manner not very different from our worship services today.
They began with a time of praise followed by prayer. Then
someone read from the law, that is, from the first five books

of the Bible. The one who had been invited to speak that day—a visiting teacher or a rabbi or a learned layperson—read a selection from the Prophets and addressed the people. It was very similar to our worship service today. They stood up to read, indicating their respect for the word of God. They sat down to preach, giving us our derivation of the old conception of the professor's chair.

The scriptures make it clear that Jesus worshiped regularly. Again and again, we find references to his going to the synagogue on the Sabbath. Luke tells us that in the beginning of his ministry he went to the synagogue "as was his custom" (4:16, NRSV) or as one translation has it, "as was his habitual practice" (Williams) or "as was his habit on the Sabbath Day" (William Barclay). A good habit like worship, when it's regular and systematic, is a wonderful practice. It is one of the habits that we promised to develop when we joined the church. We said, "I will support the church with my presence." Richard Weaver has reminded us of the importance of regular attendance at worship by saying that habits are like cables in that we weave a thread of them every day and finally we cannot break them. How is it, then, since this was the habitual practice of our Lord, that in our country we see worship attendance declining? Just in case you may be thinking that this question does not need to be raised with you but should be addressed to the absentees, let me cite an experience from my boyhood on the farm.

Occasionally, we would try to catch all of the hogs on our farm in order to treat them with some awful concoction that was designed to keep the critters (ticks, fleas, and so forth) off of them. We would put this treatment on them, and my father would always say, "Now, boys, remember there will be some of them that you cannot catch, so put an extra dose on those you do catch. Sooner or later they will rub up against the others." I have always had that attitude about preaching, because I feel that, in a real sense, those who are

22

present are our conduit to the absentees. They are the connection with all of those persons for whom worship is not a priority. Moreover, a recent Gallup Poll indicates that we have to address the church people, even those who have taken a vow, because 70 percent of today's church members feel they can be good members without going to church (*Houston Post,* June 24, 1989).

Some say the reason for our decline in attendance is as old as the parable of the sower. Perhaps church attendance is down because of our overcrowded lives. We have so many options today. We do not mean to neglect worship. If someone said, "Are you going to reject God?" we would say, "Heavens, no." We, like the weeds in the parable of the sower, slowly crowd our lives until there isn't any room for the good seed to grow; there is no time for worship.

I had an experience once that illustrates how we can overcrowd our lives. I had gone to preach a revival—a much-publicized revival. A gracious lady had been delegated the responsibility of meeting my plane. She said to me, "I am so thrilled that you have come to preach our revival and that you are going to be in our church this week." She then added, "I will not be in attendance, however, because I am too busy, but I just want you to know that I will be thinking about you." I thought, if we could rope in all of those people who think about us, we would be four deep in the church every time we meet.

You will remember that our Lord said that when he comes again, it will be as in the days of Noah. People will be eating, drinking, marrying, and giving in marriage. What is wrong with that? Nothing. That is the very stuff that life is made of, but it is stuff that crowds God out if we are not deliberate, disciplined, and intentional.

We never lose our faith suddenly. Not many of us are in danger of being swallowed by a whale in one gulp, but we are ultimately in danger of being nibbled to death by minnows. Faith goes gradually.

I have a friend who, with his wife, went to the Bahamas not long ago for a marvelous holiday. During their visit, they went to the outdoor marketplace and saw people buying and selling. My friend was all eyes and took in everything. He even saw a mouse nibbling out of a bag of corn meal. When he saw the mouse, he made a comment to his wife, and the proprietor of the stall overheard him. She snapped at him, "The mouse has got to eat, too, you know." My friend thought that she said it pretty well. All God's creatures have to eat.

But what if we take the attitude of "everything has to eat" toward everything that is nibbling and corrosive about us? Suppose we say about one mouse eating off our plate, "Oh, what difference does one mouse make?" What difference will two make or a hundred or two hundred? What do we do about the insidious encroachments of all that would secularize us and tell us that the worship of God is not a requirement, that our worship of Almighty God is an elective? We will go when we feel like it. We will go when nothing else is going on. Some people have worship crowded out of their agendas. For others, it is an afterthought. It is not really a priority. They could be in worship if it ever became a priority.

The following story occurred while I was in my first church, a student appointment with fewer than one hundred members. I kept encouraging a neighbor, who had a large family, to bring her children to Sunday school. She kept giving me excuses. She told me she could not possibly get all of her children ready for Sunday school. Her house was bedlam. She would get one cleaned up, and before she could get the next one ready, the first one would get dirty again. She always had to cook breakfast because her husband would not help. I was naive in those days. I really thought it was impossible for her to attend. I set my clock at six o'clock one Sunday morning and knocked on her back door at 6:30. She came stumbling to the door, pulling her robe around her. She had curlers in her hair. She had not put on any makeup. She looked just like any person would who wakes up in the middle of the night. I said, as I took off my coat and rolled up my sleeves, "Do you want me to bathe the babies or do you want me to cook breakfast?" She said, "I really want you to go home." She said, "If you will go home, I will be in Sunday school." From that day on they were regular in Sunday school. It became a holy habit in their lives. I discovered in that experience that it had been a possibility for her all of the time. It just had not been a priority.

I think the Jews are right when they say that the Sabbath should begin at sundown on the day before. For people who do not view worship as an afterthought, that is a good time to begin. That is the time to lay out the clothes, to get the shoes polished, to study the lessons, to get the Bibles in place, to locate the offering envelopes. That is the time to prepare, so that when we go to worship it has some pointed meaning and purpose and our little ones know it is viewed with great importance.

Of course, there are also those who not only see worship as an afterthought, but also who say, "I can worship anywhere." They are correct—we can worship anywhere. Jesus said that the Father seeks those who will worship him in spirit and in truth. That can occur anywhere. You do not have to go to a church with all the symbols of faith, great music, and the like. You can worship anywhere. I hear people saying, "Pastor, I can worship on the golf course." I think they probably have a point there. I have heard the name of God regularly on the golf course. It is used right up there as often as you would hear it mentioned in church. It is not in the same context and spirit, mind you, but I hear the name of God a lot on the golf course. I have to say the way most of us play, however, it is a supreme spiritual test to go eighteen holes without absolutely losing your temper. People say they can worship anywhere, but I always wonder if they really do. Jesus worshiped everywhere. He worshiped among the lilies and the flowers of the fields. He pointed out how God spoke to him through all of nature. But Jesus was grounded in God by a weekly trip to public worship on the Sabbath. It was never either/or for him. It was both/and. How can we do any less?

Another reason for our declining attendance may be that some people have anemic ambitions. Their ambition is so limited. They do not really want very much out of life. They do not feel the necessity of coming to worship because they do not know anything about the height, depth, and breadth of God's love—of being rooted and grounded in God. They do not think big like that. A lot of people think only of the material, and for them the test of whether or not someone has been successful is how many toys they have accumulated at the time of their death. Do they have more toys and acquisitions than anybody else? That is their test. And so, they do not understand Christians who have a sense of the intangible. We realize that, as Christians, the unseen world defines and explains the physical world for us.

Have you ever talked to somebody about church and had them tell you that they are as decent as anybody else? If that is all people want to be, then I guess they can be satisfied. You can be decent without the church. A locomotive does not stop rolling the minute you shut off the power. A bell does not stop ringing the instant you stop pulling the rope. A turnip does not shrivel the minute you take it out of the earth. We have people all over who are running off the residue of Grandpa's, Grandmother's, or their parents' religion, and they have retained enough morality to be decent, to be respected. They will never be put in jail. The only problem is, what will happen to the next generation because nobody is passing religion on to them?

Then there are the people who say that the church is imperfect, and they delight in pointing to its imperfections. They are the "church alumni." Of course, they don't realize that if the church were perfect, then they could not get in. It would mess things up if they did. The church is imperfect and is always open to the charge of being hypocritical. This is true because our reach always exceeds our grasp. We know we are not perfect, but "we follow after." Our goal is to be spiritually perfect. We want to be conformed to the image of Jesus Christ, and so we can always be called hypocrites—because our aspirations are much higher than the realities of our lives.

How do you think Jesus kept on going to the synagogue in that mean little town of Nazareth? The people in Nazareth thought the Gentiles were fuel for the fires of hell, and Jesus knew that he was to be the Savior of the whole world. Do you think it ever grated on him to listen to the imperfect sermons? Do you think that the services in Nazareth were perfect? Do you think that they always did what was pleasing to Jesus as he was growing up to the age of thirty? Still, he was always among the people of God. He went in spite of the imperfections. When the people of God met, he was going to be among them.

Now I realize, of course, that some of the finest Christians are those whose infirmities keep them from attending public worship. I never go into our sanctuary, empty or full, that I do not think about all of the people whose prayers are with us every time we meet. They watch our televised services; some of them even dress up to watch services on Sunday. They share communion at home. I am not talking about these people. I am talking about those who deliberately turn their back on a practice Jesus himself followed.

Public worship is one of our greatest legacies. Some of us are fortunate enough to have grown up in families like that of Jesus. Jesus did not go to the synagogue the first time because he knew he was God's Son. He went because he was subject to Mary and Joseph, and they went to worship. He went because his parents took him. I have a friend who says that he thought for a long time that he had to hold up his hand to go into the church. His earliest memory as a toddler was holding his mother's hand when he went into the church. That is a tremendous legacy, and many of us are blessed to have it.

We also have a legacy of worship because we are Americans. Robert McCracken said that we must always remember that our forebears crossed the Atlantic, not to find soil for plows, but liberty for souls. They boarded their ships reading from the Bible. When they first set sail, they were reading from Hebrews about looking for a city whose builder and maker is God. The freedom of worship is our heritage, our legacy as Americans. As we watched on T.V. and saw those students in Beijing, China, being shot or hauled away from the base of those monuments and heard them singing "A Mighty Fortress Is Our God," we were sobered by the realization that worship is a great legacy for us as Americans, one that we cannot take for granted. Worship is the way we remain centered on God, and every person needs that regular centering.

Samuel Johnson wrote a book entitled *The Life of John Milton*. In that book, he talked about the Christian faith as Milton saw it. He said that a religion in which many of its rewards are distant, animated by intangibles such as faith, hope, and love, will glide (notice the word) by degrees out of one's mind unless it be invigorated and reimpressed by external ordinances and calls to worship. Not only do we need to be centered, we must be centered regularly. Every good habit is only days away from being broken. The worst habit is only three days away from being reestablished. We need the constant reimpressing that worship gives us. We need renewal. If our Lord needed renewal, how much more do we?

In his book *Anatomy of an Illness*, Norman Cousins tried to find Pablo Casals's secret for dealing with his pain. Casals was in his nineties when Cousins was writing about him. A Spanish conductor, composer, and famous cellist, Casals loved the religious works of Bach and was a well-known interpreter of them. Cousins, talking about this man who had all of the infirmities that a ninety-six-year-old tends to have, said that Casals, stooped with arthritic pain, in the mornings struggled into his studio and began to play musical compositions of Bach. As he played, the pain lessened for him and he stood a little bit more erect. Cousins discovered Casals's secret. The man had something to celebrate.

That is what occurs for us every Lord's day. We have something to celebrate. We celebrate the story of our great redemption in Jesus Christ. As we celebrate, our shoulders straighten and our pain subsides and we walk out into a difficult world more erect and confident, knowing that our God has conquered. The bad will not last. God will always prevail. Christ has conquered.

But we must remember that we do not worship just because of our need to be focused, centered, and renewed. We worship because of the divine example. Jesus worshiped. It was one of the commandments of his people. It was at the core of the covenant. "Remember the sabbath day, and keep it holy" (Exod. 20:8). Keep it set apart. It is the one day we do not have. It is set apart for worship and for rejuvenation, physically and spiritually, and we cannot neglect it. Isn't it interesting that the striking phrase "as was his custom," occurs only twice in all of the scriptures? It is used to describe Jesus' practice of going to worship on the

*we know who we belong to
to be set apart.*

29

Sabbath. It was used again to describe his going to Gethsemane, his place of prayer. How can we follow Jesus to Bethlehem at Christmas? How can we follow him to Joseph's Garden at Easter and not follow him to church on the Sabbath? You and I must ultimately deal with the divine example.

Did you see the movie *Places in the Heart,* set in Waxahachie, Texas? I like that movie. It starts in a church and the members are singing, "This is my story, this is my song." It ends in the same church. In between, Sally Fields' husband is killed, her hired man is beaten up and driven away, and she nearly loses her farm, but in the end they are back in the little church having communion. The husband who has been killed is there, and the man who killed him is there, all of them together. As you watch it, you realize there is a great power of redemption in this world and we cannot defeat that power. When we worship, when it becomes our story, we align ourselves with that power, and we share in the victory of Jesus Christ.

3

SACRAMENTS

The Means of Grace

For I received from the Lord what I also handed on to you, that the Lord Jesus on the night when he was betrayed took a loaf of bread, and when he had given thanks, he broke it and said, "This is my body that is for you. Do this in remembrance of me." In the same way he took the cup also, after supper, saying, "This cup is the new covenant in my blood. Do this, as often as you drink it, in remembrance of me." For as often as you eat this bread and drink the cup, you proclaim the Lord's death until he comes. (I Cor. 11:23-26)

The telephone rang with that ominous sound it always makes when it rings at three o'clock in the morning. Following my sleepy "hello," a voice on the other end of the line identified herself as a nurse in the intensive care unit of a local hospital. She was calling on behalf of a ninety-six-year-old parishioner who was making a request of her pastor.

I had visited this elderly church member earlier and knew she was seriously ill, but I did not foresee an imminent crisis. In reality, the nurse explained, the church member was experiencing a spiritual crisis involving doubt, and she was requesting the Lord's Supper in the intensive care unit at three o'clock in the morning

After our four o'clock communion service, this church

member explained how, as she was lying there that morning, she had been tempted to doubt her experience of salvation. "I called you," she said, "because I needed the assurance that comes only through the Lord's Supper."

As I drove back to the parsonage following our unusually early communion service, I was impressed once more by the necessity of the Lord's Supper as a means of grace. I also understood why the scripture in I Corinthians 11 is so precious.

The Corinthian passage is crucial not only because it is a part of the word of God, a record of the self-revelation of God, but also because it is the earliest account of the institution of the Lord's Supper. It's the first time the Church is given explicit directions in written form about celebrating the Lord's Supper. It is even more special because it is the first recording of the words of Jesus anywhere in the Bible, even earlier than in the Gospel accounts. So this passage marks a first in several ways. More than that, this scripture confirms what we already knew about Jesus. Our Lord was not too concerned with establishing all kinds of rites and ordinances. As a matter of fact, he established only two: baptism and the Lord's Supper, or Holy Communion. Baptism is to be experienced once in your life: "one Lord, one faith, one baptism" (Eph. 4:5). The Lord's Supper is to be celebrated as "often as you will." It is a continuing sacrament. (We will discuss the sacrament of baptism in the chapter on fellowship.)

The Lord's Supper, Jesus says, should be celebrated continuously and should be one of our holy habits. "Do this," he said, and in the Greek language the command is continuous. "Do this," he said, "until I come again." In other words, the Lord's Supper has an interim character about it. We celebrate the Lord's Supper knowing that in the new order we will feast at the Messianic banquet. The Lord's Supper is an interim celebration reminding us of what was, what is now, and what is going to be. Jesus says quite clearly, "For as often as you eat this bread and drink the cup, you proclaim the Lord's death until he comes" (I Cor. 11:26).

This memorial, which is to be to all generations, was obviously taken very seriously by the early Church. Many people ask how often the early Church celebrated the sacrament of Holy Communion. In the second chapter of Acts, we read that from the very beginning the first Christians devoted themselves to the apostles' teaching, to fellowship, to the breaking of bread, and to prayers. In other words, this sacrament of the Lord's Supper was a holy habit for the early Christians, just as today's Christians are called to the same practice.

New Testament scholar Leander Keck has declared that the early Christians celebrated the Lord's Supper each time they met, whether it was daily, twice a week, or weekly. Any time they came together, they celebrated the Lord's Supper. He said that the only time there was a separation between the word and the table or between the sermon and the sacrament, the only time they did not have both, was when there was no preacher present to consecrate the elements of the Lord's Supper. That same tradition marked us in this country as Christianity made its advent here.

John Wesley sent the Sunday evening service to America and told his preachers to follow it. The Sunday service contains a provision for the celebration of the Lord's Supper every time Christians worship. Wesley did not understand the situation in America as well as Francis Asbury. America did not have educated clergy. Ninety or ninety-five percent of the preachers were laypeople, and they were circuit riders. There were no churches, but rather "preaching places." The people who came to those "preaching places" had to wait until an elder came, such as Asbury or one of the others who had the authority to consecrate the elements. The frequency with which the Christians enjoyed the Lord's Supper depended upon whether or not there was an ordained elder present.

Recently one of our seminary presidents wrote an article entitled "Can You Have a Faith Movement and an Educated Clergy?" For a long time in this country, famous preachers such as Peter Cartwright argued against it. He said that we cannot have a faith movement and an educated clergy. The seminary president who wrote the article says that the question is still open; we do not yet know whether we can have a faith movement and an educated clergy. Well, in the days of Francis Asbury they had a faith movement and they did not have the educated clergy, so they could not have the sacrament as often as we have it today.

In our church in Houston we have people from many different denominations who are a part of our fellowship. Some are from denominations that celebrate the Lord's Supper on every Lord's Day. Consequently, in our chapel we offer communion before the first service and at the end of the last service. Then, on a regular basis we offer communion to all the worshipers in the sanctuary.

Why is it that communion has lost popularity in some churches? When the announcement is made that they are going to have communion, many churches experience their lowest attendance. Some members will say, "I am not going to church today; they are not going to have preaching; they are just going to have communion." People do not recognize that this sacrament preaches its own powerful sermon.

In a dramatic way the sacrament represents, as often as we partake, Jesus Christ until his coming again. We proclaim the message and accept what Christ has done all over again. It is not just a declaration of what God has done. That is what the Jews do with the Passover Feast. When

Jews meet to celebrate the Passover, they remember how their forebears took the Passover lamb and sprinkled its blood on the doorpost of their homes in Egypt, so that when the Angel of Death came to their house, he "passed over." The Lord delivered them that night in Egypt. They remember what God has done. But when Christians come to this celebration, we do not come to a memorial to a dead hero; we do not just remember what God has done, rather we meet a risen Christ. We meet a living Lord at this table, and through his Spirit we appropriate by faith the work he did for us in his atoning death on the cross. The sacrament makes real, puts into time and space, the activity of God in Jesus Christ.

We have two things at the center of our service. We have a cross, and we have a table. It is not just a memory of something that once was; it is a promise of what he is doing now. It is a promise of what he can do in your life.

Oh, I know we have our differences about the theology of the Lord's Supper. I hate to see churches get all crossed up because of their different theologies. No one has ever been able to totally explain what happens in the Lord's Supper. Some maintain that when appropriate persons pray over the bread and the wine, it becomes the body and the blood of Jesus in a literal sense. Many of us wonder how that could be. Jesus was holding the bread in his hand when he said, "This is my body." Since he was in his body, how could the bread be his body at the same time? We offer the theory and the theology that this is a faith transaction. We receive the body and blood as symbols. By faith they become Christ for us. Now that does not make Jesus any less real. He can be as real spiritually as anyone can be physically. Luther, who argued for the faith transaction, said that Jesus was so real in the sacrament that he crunched him between his teeth as he bit the bread. Like Luther, we believe Christ is really present, but we believe the miracle is not changing bread into flesh, but the miracle is what happens in the heart of the believer. The heart is where the miracle takes place.

Perhaps you have read about the marathoner Eric Liddell, whose story inspired the movie *Chariots of Fire*. Eric Liddell ran in the 1924 Olympics and won the gold medal in the 400 meters. He was a strong, devoted Christian and refused to race on Sunday. The race had to be rescheduled at another time as he would not participate on the Lord's Day. Right after that Olympic event he went to China as a missionary and died there in a prisoner-of-war camp during the Second World War. Eric Liddell, who was known for his powerful finishes, was once asked how he could stumble at the beginning of a race—or even fall down—and still get up and win the race. The one who asked the question perhaps thought that Liddell would give him some special technique or training maneuver that enabled him to finish with such power. Instead, Eric Liddell declared that his strength to finish came from within.

That is the way it is with a Christian. We come to the Lord's Supper not expecting some kind of magic, but knowing that if we come in the right spirit and if we come with faith, it is like accepting Jesus all over again. We come out of the experience with something having happened within us. We have found a new strength.

We discover in the sacrament what John declares in his Gospel, that this Jesus is really the Bread of heaven. Not like the manna in the wilderness that the children of Israel ate and soon hungered for again, Jesus has come down from heaven to be the bread that lasts and saves the whole world. He says, "The bread that I will give for the life of the world is my flesh" (John 6:51). United Methodists believe that this bread from heaven ought to be available to all people, so we practice open communion. Whosoever will may come, if they meet the following qualifications: "if you are sorry for your sins and are in love and charity with your neighbors and intend to lead a new life."

Why is our communion open? Because people like Wesley decided that the Lord's Supper is a means of grace (as it was for my friend in the hospital). God works through this sacrament. God changes people's lives when they come to this sacrament. So why shouldn't it be open to all people who need to be changed? Besides, who is good enough to decide who is worthy and who isn't?

Paul had a problem with the Corinthians concerning worthiness. He said that some of them were not charitable. They were scrambling for all of the food and all of the best seats. They had a love feast like our covered-dish suppers at the same time that they had the Lord's Supper. The rich people got there early, however, and crowded into the dining room and got all of the good food, and the slaves and the poor people had to stay out in the atrium or courtyard and eat the scraps. Paul said, "For all who eat and drink without discerning the body, eat and drink judgment against themselves" (I Cor. 11:29). We are all one when we come to the table of Jesus and we are as brothers and sisters "in love and charity with [our] neighbors" ("Invitation," *United Methodist Hymnal*, p. 26). Who can decide? If you think you are worthy, you are not worthy.

A minister friend of mine tells about a woman who came to his study one day and wanted to receive Holy Communion. In this minister's faith tradition you examined the communicant prior to communion. He started trying to examine the poor woman, who had never been to school a day in her life. He would ask her the questions and she would hesitate and stumble; she could not answer them. She had a horrible time in her examination. Finally, the minister told her that he could not give her the Lord's Supper. She turned and walked to the door of his office, and just before she left, she turned and told him that although she could not speak for her Lord, she could die for him. The minister broke with his tradition. He told the woman that she should come back; he gave her the sacrament. If this sacrament says anything, it says God is for us—the unworthy, the sinner—he is for us. Jesus said, "This is my body, which is given for you" (Luke 22:19). Have you learned that about God?

My wife and I recently attended a high school reunion. Even after all of these years, one of the women in my graduating class still makes me feel a little bit uncomfortable. During our school days, she seemed to delight in telling the teacher about my activities. She was always trying to get me in trouble. Although many years had passed since her tattling got me in trouble with the teacher, I still felt uncomfortable around her. In some ways, I grew up feeling like that toward God. I was told he loved me, but I thought he was really trying to get something on me. It was a long time before I comprehended the fact that "God did not send the Son into the world to condemn but in order that the world might be saved through him" (John 3:17). Now what kind of difference does that make in your life? When God told Moses, "Moses, I am for you" (Von Rad), Moses had to go back and face the Pharaoh. He felt empowered to face the greatest ruler in the world at that time. That is what this sacrament declares. This sacrament says that the God who is for us can give us the strength to live for him.

I shall never forget the cold February morning in 1968 when I knelt at the chancel in Old Durham Chapel at Candler School of Theology to receive Holy Communion. As soon as my table had been served, I stood up to go down the center aisle to return to my pew. I had not taken more than a few steps when I saw Mrs. Helen Stowers standing in the back of the chapel waving in my direction. When I reached the back of the chapel, she shared the tragic news that my father-in-law had been killed in a hunting accident.

I left school immediately to drive more than two hundred miles to Douglas, Georgia, in order to be with my wife, her mother, and our family. All of the way during that drive and in the years since, I have remembered that I was prepared for whatever might come through receiving the holy sacrament. We never know what will greet us after we leave the table. We believe, however, that no matter what comes, with Christ in us we are able to face it.

We forget that not only is Jesus likened to the Lamb that was slain for sin, but also he is likened to the Paschal lamb. What is the difference? The people did not eat the lamb given for a sin offering, but they ate the Paschal lamb because it was to nourish and to strengthen the people. Jesus is the Paschal Lamb. He is the strengthener of his people. He called himself "The Bread of Life."

I heard an Armenian describe the bread of life. I had never heard it said like he put it. He said that Westerners do not understand what Jesus was saying when he said, "I am the Bread of Life." You see, in the Middle East, bread is not just something extra thrown in at a meal. It is the heart of every meal. They have those thin pieces of pita bread at every meal. Those strict people would not think about taking forks and putting them in their mouths. To put an object in your mouth defiles it. You certainly would not take a fork out and put it in again and go on defiling yourself like that. Instead, you break off a piece of the bread, pick up your food with it and eat it. Indeed, the only way you can get to the main dish, he said, is with the bread. Jesus was saying that the only way you can come to life is through him. That is what he was saying—I am the Bread of Life; I am the only way to come to life. Every time we receive the Lord's Supper, we recognize that truth all over again.

Alfred Noyes said in his autobiography that if he were ever tempted to doubt the authenticity of his Christian faith, one memory would push all of his doubts aside. That memory was the look on his father's face when he left the table of Holy Communion. The Church has been given a treasure. The Church alone is the custodian of the institution of the Lord's Supper. When we leave the table, we go with that radiant strength that is ours when we know that Christ is for us, Christ is within us, giving us courage and the will to live life as he would have us live it.

4

— FELLOWSHIP —

The Protective Circle

As it is, there are many members, yet one body.

If one member suffers, all suffer together with it; if one member is honored, all rejoice together with it. Now you are the body of Christ and individually members of it. (I Cor. 12:20, 26-27)

One afternoon I visited a friend who is a faithful viewer of our televised worship service. My friend, who has a marvelous sense of humor and a bright spirit, has Lou Gehrig's disease. She has a permanent tracheotomy and has been on a breathing machine for twenty-seven years. I asked her how she had maintained her sunny disposition and love of life. She pointed upward and said, "By the help of our heavenly Father." Then she began to name her nurses, her family, and her Christian friends. As I looked at her bright smile and heard her speak with great difficulty through a special device, I understood the secret of her great strength: her faith in God and a loving, caring circle of Christian friends.

If we were searching for the perfect picture of the church in its essential unity—a caring circle of friends—we would be hard pressed to find one more accurate or compelling than the one that Paul presents in the twelfth chapter of

I Corinthians. It sounds so elementary in its basic truth. The church, this body of Christ of which we are a part, has many members, many different parts, and yet we are all one, even as the body is one. We cannot feel inferior or independent of one another because even the part that is considered least important is in fact indispensable to the working of the entire body. This body, Paul says, is interdependent. The eye cannot say to the hand, "I do not have any need of you," and the head cannot say to the foot, "I do not need you." What if all of the body were an ear? What if the entire body were an eye? One might say that is so basic—everyone understands that. Still, I think it may be just so elementary that the Church is often in danger of forgetting it.

You and I were confirmed not only into a faith, but also into a fellowship. When we came into the church, we were confirmed into the faith and fellowship of all true disciples of Jesus Christ. The moment we were confirmed we were initiated into a fellowship described by a beautiful word in the New Testament, *koinonia*. Most churches of any size have a Koinonia class. The word gets at the heart of the New Testament. It is a word that refers to a close, intimate relationship into which Christians enter. The word is used no less than eighteen times in the New Testament.

Christian fellowship, the close intimate relationship of Christians, is different from relationships within the world. First John tells us that we have fellowship with God the Father and with his Son, Jesus Christ. Ours is a fellowship permeated by the larger fellowship of Christ and our heavenly Father. To become a part of the Church, to be confirmed, is to be initiated into a fellowship.

Now and again people say to me, "I want to be baptized." And I say, "I am so glad you want to join the church." And they say, "But I do not want to join the church; I just want to be baptized." I always reply, "There is no such thing as a solitary believer. That is a contradiction in terms. When we are baptized, we are baptized into a company of believers. We are not just baptized without a spiritual address. We are baptized into a company of persons. When we are baptized, we are marked as Christian disciples. We receive the seal of God at our baptism. We are marked and identified as Christian disciples. Through the power of the Holy Spirit we are initiated into the Body of Christ—past, present, and future—that is the Church."

Baptism is not a human possibility. If it were, we would all find a consecrated creek every afternoon and jump into it. Baptism is something that God does. Consequently, the Methodists do not rebaptize persons. Baptism is the work of God. To rebaptize is to question the work of God. Usually, after those persons who are requesting rebaptism hear its meaning explained, they understand that they really need to recommit themselves, not question God's work.

God, through the mysterious power of the Holy Spirit, incorporates us into the Body of Christ and accepts, loves, and redeems us. As an outer sign that the Spirit has done his inner work, we receive baptism that confirms our entrance into the Body of Jesus Christ. Therefore, we all have a similar pilgrimage—"one Lord, one faith, one baptism" (Eph. 4:5).

Oh, it differs in some particulars, but we have the same story. That is why our forebears in the faith called each other "Brother" and "Sister," because we all have the same story. That is why the baptismal font is well located when it is in the narthex of a church. Every time we see it, coming in and going out of the church, we are reminded that we all come through baptism into the Body of Christ. We were baptized into a fellowship. Our baptism is a constant reminder that Christianity is a social religion.

There is a little verse about finding a home for our souls: "A place where water is not thirsty and bread loaf is not a stone. I think I came upon something, and I know that I am not wrong, that nobody, but nobody can make it all alone." As Christians, we recognize that we cannot make it all alone. We acknowledge that we have a need for other people.

It goes all the way back to the creation of the race. It goes back to the beginning, to the time when God recognized it was not good for Adam to be alone. Now that scripture does not tell us that everyone has to marry. Not everyone does marry. Most of the disciples of Jesus probably were not married.

Still, the first thing Jesus did when he started his ministry was to create a community. He created a fellowship of twelve. Before he began to write his lessons on their hearts, before he began to teach them, before he began anything, he called them into community. He knew without that protective circle around them, without that human reinforcement, the lessons would not take and their strength would be lost.

I have always had a real interest in the honey bee. When I was a boy, I was fascinated to see my father actually holding a bee in his hand without getting stung. When I asked how he could do that, he explained that he was holding a drone bee—one incapable of stinging. A short time later, I ran screaming into the house sobbing to my father that I had caught the "grownest" bee I could find and he had stung me!

A naturalist wrote a story about bees recently that was most intriguing. One of the things he said about the honey bee was that you always keep bees, you never keep a single bee. If you isolate a bee, you can give it the most favorable temperature for a bee, you can give it plenty of water and plenty of food, an ideal habitat, but the bee will die within two to three days. There is something about the community of bees that keeps it alive. You can keep bees, but you cannot keep a bee.

The same thing is true about a Christian. You can work with and worship with and be a pastor to Christians, but not a Christian. There is no such thing as a solitary Christian. That is a contradiction in terms because wherever a Christian is, even put into some of the most hostile, the most alien places in the world, that Christian begins to look for and to find, by God's grace, some Christian fellowship.

I remember the story of the German bishop who was about to preach one Sunday in the summer of 1944. He was in his study putting the finishing touches on his sermon when the Nazis arrived. He knew he was going to a dungeon. He said that when they threw him into the cell on that hot August afternoon and the steel door slammed shut behind him he had to fight to keep from losing control. He did not know if he would ever come out alive. He did not know if he would ever see the sunshine again. He said that it was an awful moment. Just as he hit the ground in that cell, he heard a sound and he went to his door and heard from another cell someone whistling "O For a Thousand Tongues to Sing." He said that he whistled the next phrase back to his unseen friend and the other prisoner whistled back. He realized in that moment as they whistled to each other that there was another One who whistled with them. Suddenly, there was a great unseen company in that place and he knew he would make it because he was still in fellowship.

Jesus encouraged us to stay in fellowship when he said, "Where two or three are gathered in my name, I am there among them" (Matt. 18:20). He calls us to be a company of believers. We are not made to be alone. We need each other.

We have different gifts to be sure. Paul had a serious problem with the Corinthian church because some of the people were proud of the gift they had received and they were lording it over the others as though their gift made them more spiritual. Paul labeled that attitude divisive and absurd. What does he say in that third verse? "No one can say 'Jesus is Lord' except by the Holy Spirit" (I Cor. 12:3). He was trying to get those people in Corinth to get out of the first grade and to go on to the mature fruits of the spirit.

That is what our Lord desires for every Christian: love, joy, peace, patience, goodness, faithfulness, gentleness, and self-control—the fruits of the Spirit. Those are the characteristics he wants the people of God to have. We come to that realization when we begin to see that God has gifted us differently in this body, but we are still one body because the spirit is one.

When I think about silly people bragging about their particular gifts, I remember, first of all, that we do not have anything we did not receive, so there is no room for boasting.

I remember some funny neighbors we had when I was a boy. They were both advanced in years, and they would meet every afternoon and tell wild stories. As a little boy, I was enthralled by them. I remember how they would get into mock arguments. One of them would say, as they were sitting on the porch, "I'm going to kick you off this porch," and the other one would say, "I'm going to bite your ear off." That kind of argument really gets a little boy's attention. However, the one who was talking about doing the kicking did not have any legs. He had lost them years before. The one who was talking about biting an ear off did not have a tooth in his head. They talked about using something they didn't have.

Sometimes when Christians begin to quibble about who has what gift, I think about my funny neighbors. We do not have anything at all until we begin to see that our gifts are given and they are given for the common good, to build up the community of faith. It is as we pool our resources that we move forward. When we come together to utilize whatever gift God has given us, then the Church becomes a powerful force for good.

In the middle of a preaching tour of Australia, Gerald Kennedy was interrupted in his sermon preparation by the maid who had come to clean his room. Kennedy said that he was grumbling when he took his chair out into the hall to study. He couldn't concentrate, however, because someone next door was practicing on the violin. He went back into his room in his impatience and the maid inquired, "Did you hear him, too?" When Kennedy asked whom she was talking about, the maid told him that there was a great concert violinist playing in rehearsal right next door and he thought maybe Kennedy had been listening to him. Gerald Kennedy quietly took his chair back out into the hall and listened to the rest of the magnificent concert. He recorded the insight gained that day in a book, saying that Christians ought to pray for the ability to see beauty in the lives around them.

We should be able to see the abilities other people have and to rejoice in them—to applaud all they can do. Every gift that has been given to the Body of Christ has been given for the purpose of service, for building up the Body. If someone's gift does not build up the Body, then we call the gift into question. It is not an authentic gift being utilized properly if it does not build up the Body of Jesus Christ. What a marvelous orchestra we are, all with different parts to play. When we come together, we are a terrific power for God.

My wife and I, on a recent trip to Florida, saw a sign just before a long bridge. The sign read, "It is against the law to run out of gas on the bridge." I do not know what you do when you get there and find that it is too late, because there are not any service stations around there. I thought it really would be pretty bad to run out of gas out there on that long two-lane bridge and cause the traffic to back up. But then I started thinking about the people whom I know that run out of gas. It ought to be against the law in the church, too, for people to run out of gas.

Invariably, when people run out of spiritual energy, it happens when they have broken fellowship, when they have forgotten the direct admonition in Hebrews 10 that talks about our not neglecting to meet together. You must meet in Bible study, in a Sunday school class, in the sanctuary. We must not neglect it, because when we meet, the Bible says that we stir one another up for love and good works. Try calling people who have been out of fellowship for a long time, who have not been "stirred up" recently, and ask them if they will make a pledge to the church and see what they tell you. Ask them if they will teach Sunday school or work with boys and girls in the youth department. Ask them if they will help on a mission work team. Ask them to do anything for Christ and his Church, and you will discover that their souls have grown cold. Like metal when it gets cold, their souls have gotten hard, is no longer soft or flexible. Something vital to the Christian life has dulled and died within them.

We held our breath when Jesus reappeared to his disciples after his resurrection and Thomas was not there. Any pastor, any Christian, would worry about Thomas. The Bible makes it plain that when Jesus came and said, "Peace be with you" (John 20:19), Thomas was not there. Why wasn't he there? Where was he? I am sure he had a good excuse. We can come up with a thousand excuses. Why were you not there the day the Spirit filled the place and the Risen Lord came? Thomas was not there. Thank goodness the Bible says that eight days later when our crucified Lord reappeared, Thomas was there. I think somebody else went out and got him. I think they said, "Thomas, if you miss him the next time, it might not matter to you two weeks from now." How many weeks can you miss Christian fellowship before it does not matter anymore? I think about Paul. He had just gotten converted when he came to the church and wanted to come in, and they would not have anything to do with him. He felt isolated. He did not know anyone in that church. No one liked him and nobody trusted him. But Barnabas, brotherly Barnabas, put his arm around Paul and loved him and believed in him. Barnabas helped get him into the fellowship. When the people who join our church come forward, I am grateful, but I do not begin to relax until they are completely into the fellowship of the church.

Once I had the opportunity to go to the Augusta National to see the Masters Tournament. The first thing I wanted to do when I got there was to follow Arnold Palmer. I knew he would not win the golf tournament. Arnold had a case of the "yips" or something with his putter, and other parts of his game had gone downhill. He was like many of us who play golf. He could still put postage on the ball, but the address was not clear. He just did not always know where it was going to wind up. I knew all of that about Arnold, but he still had that charisma, a special appeal, and I wanted to follow him. On Number 13 on the back side, Arnold yanked one down into the edge of the creek. I thought there would be no way he could get it out and far enough down the fairway to par that hole. I turned to the person beside me and decided I would explain Arnold's predicament. I proceeded to do so: "Look at Arnold; he is in a real mess. What he really needs to hit is a short iron to be safely out of there because if he hits a long iron he may not get out or he may go too far and be in trouble again and be out of bounds." That person looked at me and said, "Is this your first trip to the Masters?" I said, "Well, yes it is, but I know a little about golf." He said, "Well, if you really knew something about it, you would know that Arnold is going to hit that ball as hard as he can and he won't go out of bounds because he is going to hit that ball straight at the crowd, at the gallery."

And sure enough, that is what he did. He slashed that ball straight at the crowd and somebody who loved him a lot more than I did got in front of that ball, and it hit him, and there was a lot of kicking and scuffling, and when the ball stopped, it was right back on the fairway! That man looked at me and said, "As long as there is a crowd at Augusta National, Arnold will never hit it out of bounds."

The church needs to be a fellowship like that. People need to know that in the church the members are going to form a fellowship circle, a protective circle, around them and the members are going to watch over their souls. They will be called when they are absent, they will be exhorted when their ardor cools, they will be stirred up, they will be challenged to become disciples who are on fire for Jesus Christ. That is not a luxury for the church. We have to do it to become an authentic fellowship.

Bishop Woodie White tells the story of a little reddish brown bird in Europe called the chaffinch bird. These birds sing like canaries, but there is a strange thing about these popular little songbirds. The people take them into their homes and after a time the little birds forget how to sing. When the little birds forget how to sing, they get sick. If you do not take them back to be with the other birds at the zoo or in the woods, or wherever they congregate, to relearn how to sing, they will get depressed and die.

We can forget how to sing. We come together as Christians that we might not grow depressed, lose our song, and die spiritually. For we are a fellowship and we reach all the way from earth to heaven. When the roll is called up yonder, we expect to be in fellowship still.

5

GIVING

The Grateful Spirit

Therefore, my beloved, be steadfast, immovable,
always excelling in the work of the Lord, because you
know that in the Lord your labor is not in vain.

Now concerning the collection for the saints: you
should follow the directions I gave to the churches of
Galatia. On the first day of every week, each of you is
to put aside and save whatever extra you earn, so that
collections need not be taken when I come. And when
I arrive, I will send any whom you approve with letters
to take your gift to Jerusalem. (I Cor. 15:58–16:3)

S aturday afternoon was a happy time in the rural
home in which I grew up. That was the time when my
parents would take all of us children to town. While
Mother and Father were shopping, we went off to the
movie. There was only one movie in our small hometown,
and we always sat through the Saturday western and
accompanying cartoon several times. My parents gave me
twenty-five cents for our trip to town and for the week. I still
recall how I broke down that impressive sum and explained
it to my friends, saying "Nine cents to get into the movie, a
nickel for a coke, a nickel for some popcorn, and a penny to
throw away!" That was a lot of money for a little boy to
spend in a single afternoon, but all of my spending left one

nickel untouched. My mother saw to it that the nickel went to church on Sunday.

I knew giving was important to my mother on the Sunday when I put my tithe into the plate and decided to take a penny back. My brother, who was seated beside me, saw me put my nickel in the plate, and also saw me take a penny out. Unfortunately, he shared that information with my mother and I could tell from her reaction that she expected my nickel to remain in the plate.

The apostle Paul was very practical in his discussions about what Christians put into the offering plate. In the fifteenth chapter of I Corinthians he spoke about the resurrection and the world to come with great clarity. He told about the nature of the resurrection and about the spiritual body that we are to have. He explained how the perishable can never inherit the imperishable and how this mortal must put on immortality. Then, abruptly—as was characteristic of him—Paul moved to the practical saying, "Now concerning the collection for the saints" (I Cor. 16:1). He began to describe to the Christians in Corinth how they were to make their offerings on the first day of the week, and to prepare for a special offering that was to be sent to the poor Christians in Jerusalem.

Paul moved from the lofty theme of the resurrection, a very deep theological discussion, to a concern for the administration and the work of the Church as it is expressed through the regular offering that Christians make when they come together on the first day of the week. One can tell that, for the apostle Paul, giving was to be a habitual act, for it was to occur every week and all of God's people were expected to participate.

Perhaps we should first say, when we talk about this whole matter of giving, that the Bible presupposes that we have something to give when we are called to be givers. The apostle Paul said that we are to set aside something according to how we have prospered. Another translation has it "as much as each can spare" (NJB). Another has it "in keeping with your income" (NIV). So this God of ours is very fair and very reasonable, as Christians are called to be proportionate in their giving. God makes it clear that we can only give if we have received. That goes almost without saying.

There is a sense, however, in which everyone can be a giver in the economy of God. We remember how Jesus said that if you have given one of his disciples even a cup of cold water it will be noted by God and you will not lose your reward.

In our church in Houston, Texas, we have work areas of ministry that persons can enjoy whether they are home-bound, whether they have wealth to share, or whether they are poor. Indeed, the very core of the power of this congregation is rooted in our prayer ministry. That work does not require one cent in the way of material goods. More than that, we have a program of evangelism that puts the responsibility for church growth squarely on the shoulders of our people. We call it the Aldersgate Club, and we maintain that every person has the time and the resources to tell other people about the love of God in Jesus Christ. So, in a real sense, everyone is a giver. Everyone can contribute to the well-being of the Church of Jesus Christ. But in I Corinthians 16:1 it is clear that Paul is talking about giving money—assuming, of course, that they have received something to give.

It is interesting that Jesus said more about money than he did about prayer. I believe we all know his estimate of prayer. We all know how he practiced the discipline, but he had more to say about money. And this from a man who, apparently, during the last three years of his life did not give any person a gift of money. He gave people other priceless gifts. He gave them their sight, their hearing, and strong legs on which to walk. He gave them freedom from sin, salvation from sin, and he gave them himself. But he did not give them money. He had no money to give.

Most of us go through those stages in life when there is nothing to give. Isn't it wonderful that our Lord demonstrated in his life that there are times when we are givers (I am sure he was a giver when he was a carpenter in Nazareth), but there are also times in our lives when we are receivers. For the last three years of his life, Jesus not only didn't give money, but he received money from the women of Galilee who followed the little band of disciples and saw to their material needs. Jesus can identify with people who are going through those times in their lives when they have to be grateful receivers, knowing by the plan and grace of God that someday they may become givers.

Many important things happened in the little church in Mansfield, Massachusetts, that my wife and I attended for one year. It was a year in our lives when I was a full-time student and we had less than we have ever had in the way of material goods. Still, the little church to which we belonged made us feel like an integral part of their congregation.

We could walk to the little United Methodist church just up the street from our apartment. It was a good thing the church was nearby, because we had long since parked our car in the garage and removed the battery. We could not afford any gasoline for the car. As I look back on those days and remember all of those Sundays when the temperature was below zero, I do not know how they heated that little church. There were not very many members. I do not know how they bought the Sunday school literature we used in our work with the Sunday school. I do not know how they paid their apportionments and all of those things. They did all of it without our help. We had only pennies but they accepted us, they loved us, and they taught us something about being grateful receivers. They even took us to their

Christmas party and gave us a gift when we could not give a gift in return. Later, I remembered those years when Jesus was not able to give, but was a grateful receiver. It is more blessed to give than to receive, but Jesus was willing to forego that blessing in order to make it possible for us to enjoy it.

The other day, a young person was in my office who desperately needed some financial help. Fortunately, I had received a letter almost on the same day from an individual who had sent a handsome check saying, "At a very low time in my life when I desperately needed some help, the First United Methodist Church was there for me and I want to pass this gift on to someone else." Here was a grateful receiver who had become a generous giver with all the blessings that come when we give.

How do we become givers? Many of us were taught to give as children. If we are fortunate, we have the same background that the apostle Paul had, except, of course, that ours is Christian. William Barclay tells us that almsgiving was very important in the home where Paul grew up. The Hebrew word for almsgiving and righteousness could be used interchangeably. It was so important to them that the only way you could show you were a good person was to be a generous person. So Paul grew up with the idea that if we have the wherewithal, God expects us to be givers.

I have already shared with you about my mother's strong feelings concerning giving. I admit that I did not get much joy from giving in those days. In fact, I resented it. I was especially incensed when I reached the grade in school when I learned fractions and discovered that I had not just been tithing all those years, but I had been double tithing! Nevertheless, I was blessed in that I grew up knowing that I was to live on 90 percent. I have never become accustomed to counting on 100 percent of anything that I receive.

My wife shares my convictions about giving, so when our children were small we made a chart to guide and motivate them both in their behavior and in their finances. We listed their allowances beside their names on the chart. We linked their allowances to their behavior and how they performed their chores around the house. The first item beside their names was their tithe—10 percent.

I can still visualize the scene that greeted me on those days when I would turn onto the little dirt street leading to our house and our children had just received their allowances. They were all spread out, running as fast as they could, kicking up the dirt under their bare feet, going with all their might toward the Busy Bee Convenience Store. In that little store, which had every kind of candy and toy and gimmick small children enjoy, they would spend their entire allowances within thirty minutes after having received them. They spent everything, that is, except their tithes. Their tithes were off limits.

You are not surprised, I'm sure, to learn that all of our children, who are now grown and have families of their own, are tithers. They are tithers now because of their own choices, but they were taught to tithe from their earliest years.

I remember a story I read about John D. Rockefeller, Sr. Someone once asked him if he tithed. He said, "Yes, I tithe. I would like to tell you how I first became a tither." He said, "When I was a little boy, I had to go to work to support my mother. The first job I had paid me $1.50. I remember bringing home that first week's pay and giving it to my mother. I remember the pride I felt when I gave her my pay. She held it in her lap and looked into my eyes. She said, 'Son, you would make me very proud if you gave a tenth or 15 cents to the Lord.'" He said, "I gave a tenth of my first pay to God and I have tithed every dollar for the rest of my life." More than that he said, "I don't believe I could have tithed on my first million if I had not first tithed on that $1.50."

Of course, he is right. We kid ourselves saying, "Oh, if I only had more." It does not work that way. It gets harder the more we have, because money gets a hold on us.

I remember hearing a minister say, "We're not concerned about someone giving his or her share of the budget; what we are really concerned about is that God gets his share of that with which he has prospered you." That is not just about growing a strong church, that's about growing a strong you. That's about growing strong Christians.

Well, you can be taught to give as a child and then you can be motivated in other ways to give. Let's face it, just having been taught as a child is often not enough. We need some motivation along the way, because we are not always going to have our mothers to reinforce our giving. We need to get beyond some of the unworthy motives of giving—unworthy motives like, "I give in order to get." It bothers me to hear people saying, "I tithe, so God is going to take care of me and all of my financial needs."

I remember a man who called me with heartbreak in his voice just a few years ago. He called me because he had been dealing in the futures market. The futures market is very, very risky from what I am told, and here was a man who had almost instantly lost all of his money. He called me with tears, not just in his eyes but in his voice, and said, "Bill, I have been a tither for years and I just got wiped out. I cannot understand it." You cannot understand it if your offering is designed to be a bribe of God, if you only give in order to get. That is an unworthy motive for a Christian. That is beneath us.

It is true, oftentimes, that God continues to bless us materially. I remember reading those lines just the other day, "There once was a man though some did count him mad, who the more he cast away, the more he had." It is true, often, that the more you give away the more you have. It is also true that you cannot outgive God. But to give only to receive is a motive unworthy of a Christian disciple. Jesus said that if you do good to other people and only do good to those who are going to do good to you, what more have you done than the sinners? If you are going to lend only to those people from whom you expect to receive, then even the sinners will want a part of that action! That is a deal you could cut with anybody. It is not worthy of Christians. Jesus tells us to give and our reward will be great in heaven—we will have spiritual rewards. Give, and you will have treasures in heaven. But how can we give unless we are motivated?

Some people are motivated out of a sense of gratitude for the Church. We all have different starting places when we first begin to be givers. Some people say, "I am thankful for the Church and I want to give something to help its work." That is Paul's appeal to the Corinthians. Peter, James, and John had asked Paul if he could help collect some money for the poor Christians in Jerusalem. Paul is saying, "Look, we Christians have to take care of each other. Our brothers and sisters have some needs and aren't you thankful to belong to a Church that helps other people? Don't you really want to help other people?" That is exactly what Paul meant. Many times people begin to give because they love a church that helps other people.

I received a letter recently from a man in our community who is not a member of our church. He sent us a check for a thousand dollars. I do not know if this man has ever been in our service of worship. I do not believe he has, but he said, "Our son had a horrible automobile accident and has been in a coma for a long time. We have been by his bed and we have been praying that somehow God would bring him out of it. We got word through some of our friends that your church was praying for us, that we were on your prayer chain. We have had constant assurance, through these people, that your church is praying for us. I want to give a gift to a church that would do that for somebody else." That is a wonderful place for many people to start. I get letters all the time from people from other cities, who come to M. D. Anderson Cancer Center or one of our other great hospitals in Houston. When they return home they write to us and say, "You need to know the kind of people and the kind of staff you have. Without their prayers and without their support, we could not have made it."

Once my wife and I went to church in Bristol, England. On our way into the church we passed another little Methodist church. We saw a handful of people creeping into its doors. I do not believe we saw anyone going into that church who was under sixty-five, seventy, or maybe even older. I thought how grateful I was for those faithful souls who kept that church together. But at the same time, I turned to a young adult who was guiding us and I asked, "Where are the children, where are the young people in this church?" She said, "They are not there. We do not have young people in our churches, only a very few, if any, because the church does not have anything for them. There are no programs for our children, there are no programs for our young people. They are not here because the church does not have anything for them."

Some people begin to give because they are impressed with the importance of extending our Christian heritage to the next generation. They don't want to have their church be like the little church at Bristol. They want to have something there for children and young people. They have had their eyes opened as to what the church does and they become grateful for it.

Many people are motivated to become givers as a result of their study of the scriptures. Before Abraham was in the scriptures, there was the concept of tithing. Jacob, while he was fleeing from the wrath of his brother, Esau, made a commitment to tithe. All of the patriarchs and prophets knew about tithing. Malachi spelled it out succinctly when he declared, "Bring the full tithe into the storehouse" (Mal. 3:10). When Jesus denounced the scribes and Pharisees and hypocrites, he nevertheless endorsed the concept of tithing when he said, "Woe to you, scribes and Pharisees, hypocrites! For you tithe mint, dill, and cummin, and have neglected the weightier matters of the law: justice and mercy and faith. *It is these you ought to have practiced* without neglecting the others" (Matt. 23:23, emphasis mine).

There are many motivations and ways to become givers. The highest motivation and the best reason to give is out of gratitude for what God has done for us in Jesus Christ.

A golfer said to me, "I was as lost as a ball in high grass and Jesus found me." When you know you are lost and life does not have any meaning, purpose, or direction and Jesus finds you and you realize that he has not only died for you, but also he has been raised from the dead to empower you to live an abundant life, then all that we do is freely done. We excel. As Paul says, we are "always excelling in the work of the Lord" (I Cor. 15:58).

Once a man came to my study and dropped a brown bag on my desk containing twenty-four thousand dollars in one hundred dollar bills. Then he explained why he was making that cash gift to the church.

For a number of years the man had been very wealthy. His life, however, and that of his family had lacked the stabilizing effect of the gospel and his priorities were confused. He fell into destructive patterns in his search for meaning and inner peace. Then the petroleum industry, upon which his wealth depended, suffered terrific reversals and my friend saw his wealth disappearing.

Facing the likely possibility of being forced into

bankruptcy, my once wealthy friend began to put one hundred dollar bills in a safety deposit box. He could not bear the thought of having nothing.

Through a succession of events, my friend experienced the life-transforming power of Jesus Christ. He gained a new focus in his life. His priorities changed, and he began to "strive first for the kingdom of God (Matt. 6:33). In his new relationship with Christ, the man explained that he could not be dishonest. More than that, he was giving 10 percent of his money to the church because he had found real security in Jesus Christ. No longer was he afraid of having nothing. If he went bankrupt, he still had Christ.

My friend's new security and gratitude, coming out of his saving relationship with Jesus Christ, has made him a great giver.

I had an amazing dream the other night. I have never had a dream like it. I dreamed about my grandmother. She had beautiful white hair, which she wore in a bun. I remember being startled as a little boy the first time I saw her as she was getting ready to go to bed, with her hair down around her nightgown, reaching to her waist. In my dream, I walked into my uncle's house where she lived. I went into the back room, her room, and there she was sitting up in her bed with her hair down around her shoulders and she said, "Well, Billy, sit down here and let's talk." The amazing thing about that dream, which was in the form of a conversation, was that Grandmother died in July of 1960. Still, every syllable and every sound were exactly and precisely as I remembered her. Of course, the brain can store all of these things. When I woke up and reflected on my dream, however, I thought: No wonder Paul could say that he was willing to trust everything to God toward that last day. Our God does not lose anything. If he can help us keep a perfect memory of the voice and looks of a loved one, nothing is lost with God.

"Your labor is not in vain," Paul told those Christians. "You do not labor in vain." Another way of saying it is, "Nothing you ever give to God is lost or wasted—nothing." Indeed, what you do for God is the only permanent thing in this world.

The pyramids are not permanent. They are going away. You don't have to jump on a plane tomorrow in order to see them because it will take a few million years for them to sink beneath the Egyptian sand. But they are not going to stay because they are sinking about an inch every few thousand years. They are not permanent. There is nothing in this world that is permanent. The only permanent thing or person in this world is the one who is rightly related to God in Jesus Christ. Nothing you give is lost or wasted if it is given in the name of Jesus Christ. That is why we delight to labor for him, to give to the Church because our labor and our giving to the Lord are never in vain.

6

— WITNESSING —

Sharing the Faith

From now on, therefore, we regard no one from a human point of view; even though we once knew Christ from a human point of view, we know him no longer in that way. So if anyone is in Christ, there is a new creation; everything old has passed away; see, everything has become new! All this is from God, who reconciled us to himself through Christ, and has given us the ministry of reconciliation; that is, in Christ God was reconciling the world to himself, not counting their trespasses against them, and entrusting the message of reconciliation to us. So we are ambassadors for Christ, since God is making his appeal through us; we entreat you on behalf of Christ, be reconciled to God. For our sake he made him to be sin who knew no sin, so that in him we might become the righteousness of God. (II Cor. 5:16-21)

During a preaching mission in India I heard a story about a Christian missionary who had managed to dig a good well of water that served a small rural community. Years after the missionary was gone, a non-Christian asked one of the villagers why he kept an old page from a newspaper hanging on the wall of his house. The villager explained that once when he had purchased some fish at the market the merchant had wrapped them in the old newspaper. When the villager opened the paper, he saw a picture of Jesus on one of the pages. "I framed that page and put it on my wall," he explained, "because that man," pointing at Jesus, "gave me clean water to drink."

Jesus must always be prominent in our lives because he has given us "living water" to drink. How effective are we in sharing Christ with others? In the city of Houston, Texas, we have just crossed a line for the first time in our history. Not since our beginning years have we had a greater percentage of our population who do not belong to a church or a synagogue than those who do. But Christians have now became a minority in the fourth largest city in the nation—a city many of us call home.

Why are we so timid about telling the gospel story? After all, as we read the Scripture, we are given to understand that our singular responsibility is to share the good news of Jesus Christ. The work of our reconciliation has already been accomplished for us by our God through Jesus Christ. It is our greatest responsibility to tell that story. What a wonderful story we have to tell! How did Alexander Maclaren say it? He said, "Love upon the throne bends down to ask of the rebel that lies powerless and sullen at his feet" (*Exposition of Holy Scripture,* vol. 14 [Grand Rapids: Baker Book House, 1975], p. 382). We have a God, who in coming to be our Savior, lowered himself, even humiliated himself, by taking the form of the lowest servant and dying an awful death on the cross that we might be saved from our sins. "For our sake he made him to be sin who knew no sin, so that in him we might become the righteousness of God" (II Cor. 5:21).

Once when a group of us from Texas was going in to see that magnificent edifice, Westminster Abbey, I looked for a long moment across the street at Westminster Central Hall, a remarkable building in its own right. Central Hall is the Methodist church at which W. E. Sangster, a great British preacher, preached for many years. As I looked at that building, I thought about Sangster and his marvelous preaching ability. I remembered one of his sermons in which he talked about the ships that used to take the garbage away from the city of London. They did not know much about the environment in those days, so they would have ships take their unredeemable garbage out to the North Sea. When the ships were positioned directly over a deep, dark hole in the sea, they would open all of the sludge gates and release the garbage into the depths of the deep, salty sea. Dr. Sangster loved to stand in the pulpit and remind the people of those ships and to ask them, "Do you have any unredeemable garbage that you want to put on the ship today? Do you have anything you want to give over to Christ? He will take it. For we have a God who has not only given us forgiveness, but he has also offered to lose our sins in the seas of forgetfulness." We have a great God who not only forgives but he forgets our sins. He remembers our iniquities no more. What a wonderful story we have to tell. Ours is a story with a happy ending. Our God loved us so much that the great became small and took on our robe of human flesh. God became like us that he in turn might make us like him.

A scripture scholar, who taught a Bible study during a recent meeting of the Texas Annual Conference, helped those of us who were present to more clearly understand the nature of God. He retold the parable of the prodigal son. In the story, he shared with us some insights that come only through a Middle Eastern background. Westerners could not begin to understand all of the nuances of the meanings of that magnificent parable. For instance, when he spoke to us about the father who was waiting, yearning, praying, and hoping for his son to come back from the far country, he described how when the father saw him at yet a great distance, he ran and embraced him. Well, we know that part of the story. We have all heard that hundreds of times. Perhaps what we did not realize is that in that culture for an adult male to run was unheard of, because the last thing a male Jew would do would be to show his ankles or the bottoms of his feet. To show the bottoms of one's feet is to insult the other persons who are near. Indeed, he told about some contemporary Orthodox Jews who were engaged in a formal colloquy with Christians and the Christians inadvertently crossed their legs, as we are prone to do, and the Jews got up and left the room. They felt insulted. You just did not do that. So when Jesus described a loving father who was so excited about seeing his son that he forget himself and was willing to become an object of derision and ridicule, to have people point at him and laugh, he was saying that the father was willing for people to think him a fool because his love constrained him to run and embrace the son who had turned once more toward home.

Is it any wonder then that the Jews call the cross a scandal? The idea of a God who would humiliate himself, who would stoop, who would become a laughingstock, was an incredible thought. We would have to agree that it is one of the greatest stories ever told.

Christ and the Church expect us to tell the story, to share our faith. When we joined the church, we were asked if we would profess our faith in Jesus Christ as Savior and Lord. We were asked if we would confess him and if we would profess the faith in the Old and New Testaments. In other words, will you make that your faith story? Will you profess it? Will you confess it? Do you know what those words mean? Those words simply mean that you will openly acknowledge and disclose Jesus as your Savior. Will you publicly claim the faith story and make it your story wherever you go as long as you live?

Indeed, standing publicly before an altar is only a preview of that which we are expected to do in the world. Never mind that the world is sometimes hostile toward our

Christ. Never mind that our materialistic values are in direct opposition to his spiritual values. Never mind that we might be unpopular because of them. We are brought to the altar of the church as a preview of what we are called to do in the world.

Paul says it plainly: "So we are ambassadors for Christ, since God is making his appeal through us" (II Cor. 5:20). Do you know who an ambassador was? In Paul's time, an ambassador was one who had been directly commissioned by the monarch. Everyone who saw an ambassador knew that he bore in his person the honor and the authority of the monarch because he had been commissioned. We have been commissioned. Through baptism, all Christians are ordained to carry in our persons the honor and the authority of our monarch. We are to represent God in whatever situation we find ourselves.

The commission of the ambassador did not end, however, with purely representing the monarch by whom the ambassador had been commissioned. The ambassador also helped new nations draw up their constitutions, and outline boundaries, and helped them come into the family of the empire. It follows, then, with this understanding of being ambassadors, that it is the responsibility of every Christian to do his or her part under direct orders from the sovereign and, through virtue of our baptism, to bring all nations into the family of God's Kingdom. The Church expects it of us, and Christ is even more explicit. How did he say it? He said it plainly to his disciples and he said it bluntly, "You shall be my witnesses" (Acts 1:8). He did not raise the question, "Would you like to be? Do you think it would be all right? Is it okay if I sign you up?" He said to all who would be his disciples, "Go therefore and make disciples of all nations, baptizing them in the name of the Father and of the Son and of the Holy Spirit, and teaching them to obey everything that I have commanded you. And remember, I am with you always, to the end of the age" (Matt. 28:19-20).

In that matchless Sermon on the Mount, Jesus said that we are the "light of the world." You do not light a candle and smother it with a bushel basket. You do not put out your light. You let it shine. At another time, he was even more direct because he told his disciples that part of following him involves acknowledging one's faith. "Everyone therefore who acknowledges me before others, I also will acknowledge before my Father in heaven; but whoever denies me before others, I also will deny before my father in heaven" (Matt. 10:32-33).

I heard someone the other day talking about a list he had for God. He had all kinds of things he wanted to ask God when he got to heaven. I think that is okay. We will all take questions with us to heaven; I am sure of that. One of the questions this person shared was quite legitimate. He said, "I want to ask God why when we pray for healing one person is healed, but ten more are not healed." This person went on to say, "I do not even know how the one, the one miraculously healed, can celebrate. How do you go around the world celebrating that you were healed when a hundred or a thousand beside you weren't healed?" He went on to say, "Maybe God miraculously heals, as he does occasionally, just to remind us of who is going to have the last word." But as this person struggled with all of the questions he was going to ask God when he got to heaven, I could not help thinking that God also has a list. We are not the only ones to have a list. God has a list, too. On God's list he is going to have all of those opportunities he gave us to say a good word for Jesus—to tell someone the old, old story. Did we tell the story? We do not have to do the reconciling. We do not have to forgive the sins, to pay the price; all of that has been done. Did we tell the story? Maybe he is going to ask, "Why was it hard for you to tell it? Was it because you did not like the idea of being a marked person?" There is a burden of expectation put on us when we claim Christ before our friends and our community.

A longtime friend of mine from south Georgia was teaching in a Christian enrichment school. I saw him at the beginning of the school year and I asked, "How are you doing?" He said, "I am exhausted." I could not believe it. I said, "What do you mean you are exhausted? You have not even had your first class yet. You are going to be teaching all week long; what do you mean you are exhausted?" He said, "So many people have signed up for my class. I am exhausted from carrying the burden of expectation."

The burden of expectation can be heavy, and when we share with those around us that we are disciples of Jesus Christ, we discover something about the burden of expectation. The spotlight is turned on us. They expect us to talk a certain way. They expect us to behave a certain way; they look at us with a new awareness, an expectancy. Many people, therefore, refuse to own the name of Christ simply because they do not want that burden on them. Some are just plain timid. They say, "I don't know enough to tell other people about Jesus."

Recently, the Houston Astros have been talking about a trade involving two baseball players. I have heard people who don't even know the batting averages of the players—let alone all of the inside information that an Art Howe, the manager of the Astros, or a Bill Wood, the general manager of the Astros, or anyone who is an expert on the subject would know—still express opinions about the trade. I have not encountered many people who don't have an opinion about baseball trades.

Where does all of our timidity come from when it comes to speaking about Jesus Christ? We don't have to know everything. We may not know enough theology to write the title on a term paper. We may be like that man whom Jesus touched and healed. The only thing we may be able to say is "All I know is that I was once blind and now I see" or "I do not know any theology, but he helped me." That might be where we start, but every Christian should have a story to tell.

We might be like that modern painter who said to the carpenter, "Do your best and I will caulk the rest." We do not have to be perfect witnesses, for we have a God who says, "You do your best and when it is over you will hear me say, 'Well done, good and faithful servant.'" We are not judged by our successes, but by our faithfulness.

Our faith requires that we witness. John Wesley wrote a letter to a new convert that one can read in The New Room at Bristol, England. In that letter he said, "To share the work of God is one of the appointed ways of retaining that which God has wrought." It is one of the appointed ways of retaining our Christian faith.

People say to me all the time, "Pastor, I am not growing spiritually; why can't I grow? Why isn't my prayer life improving?" One of the reasons we cannot grow is because God cannot get more of his Spirit into us until he can get his Spirit out of us. It is like electricity. If you want to grow in your faith, you must learn how to share your faith. You'd better learn how to give faith away if you want to get more faith. It is true that there is no such thing as secret discipleship, because either the secret takes away the discipleship or the discipleship takes away the secret. We can moan and groan because we are not growing in our prayer life, but the reason for our failure to grow may be because we are not sharing the faith. A vital faith requires witnessing. Our own story requires it. "I love to tell the story, it did so much for me; and that is just the reason I tell it now to thee" (*The United Methodist Hymnal*, 156).

I never come to the beginning of a new school year without remembering the circumstances in which I started to college for my first semester. My father had turned thumbs down on my decision to enter the ministry. I took my suitcase and hitchhiked to the nearest junior college. Along the way, I cried. As I walked along, crying and feeling sorry for myself, however, I thought back over the past few days and came to the realization that I would not trade the peace I had found for the approval of any person in the world, including that of my own father. For you see, a little while before that, I met Jesus Christ in a grove of pine trees outside our country home. He spoke to my heart, and for the first time in my life, I yielded to him. I said, "All right, Lord, I will go where you want me to go; I will say what you want me to say; and I will be what you want me to be." From that day to this, I can sing that old refrain, "Gone, gone, gone, gone, all my sins are gone." I can take my sins to someone who will not only forgive them, but also will forget them. My own story compels me to share the love of Jesus. Do we believe what we say we believe?

A friend sent me a bulletin about a man who was getting up a petition for the city council against a church. He said the church was too noisy. People were too enthusiastic. He took the petition to a Jewish neighbor and thought he would be the first to sign it. The neighbor read the petition, looked at the man, and said that he could not sign the petition. He said that if he believed what those people believe, that their Savior has come, he would probably be noisier than they are. Do we believe that our Savior has come? Do we believe that he has become sin that we might become righteous?

One Sunday night I went to the altar of our church. Hundreds go to the altar each week. Thousands through the years have come to our altar. I came during prayer time as the lights were dimmed. I came to say my prayers and when I knelt, I was surprised. I should not have been, but I was. The altar rail where I knelt was wet with the tears of the person who had preceded me there. I don't know who it was, but the rail was wet with tears. For some reason I believed that those tears were shed for another. I asked myself as I saw the wet rail, "When was the last time I cried over the plight of a lost and a lonely person? Our God expects every Christian to "weep o'er the erring one, lift up the fallen, tell them of Jesus, the mighty to save" (*The United Methodist Hymnal*, 591).

7

BIBLE READING

Growing a Soul

But as for you, continue in what you have learned and firmly believed, knowing from whom you learned it, and how from childhood you have known the sacred writings that are able to instruct you for salvation through faith in Christ Jesus. All scripture is inspired by God and is useful for teaching, for reproof, for correction, and for training in righteousness, so that everyone who belongs to God may be proficient, equipped for every good work.

In the presence of God and of Christ Jesus, who is to judge the living and the dead, and in view of his appearing and his kingdom, I solemnly urge you: proclaim the message; be persistent whether the time is favorable or unfavorable; convince, rebuke, and encourage, with the utmost patience in teaching. For the time is coming when people will not put up with sound doctrine, but having itching ears, they will accumulate for themselves teachers to suit their own desires, and will turn away from listening to the truth and wander away to myths. (II Tim. 3:14–4:4)

My nephew Michael enjoyed a close relationship with his pediatrician. Long after Michael's friends had graduated to a regular physician, Michael continued to rely on his pediatrician. A large boy for his age, Michael went to see his pediatrician one day for a pre-school check-up and found himself sitting in a room full of toddlers and infants. While they were waiting, a little child, just beginning to learn to speak, started walking around a circle of patients, touching each baby on its knee. As the little toddler touched each child, he would say in that beautiful baby voice, "Bay Bee, Bay Bee." One after the other he touched the infants until he came to Michael. When he saw a tall, gangling pre-teen boy, he touched his knee as well and said, "Bigggg Bay Bee." Michael promptly got another doctor!

If you are to grow as a Christian into the full stature of Jesus Christ, you must attend to one of the ordinances of God that John Wesley considered necessary for Christian living—the daily practice of reading the scriptures. Paul maintains that a thorough understanding of the scripture is necessary in order to be useful to God or to be complete and equipped for good work (II Tim. 3:17).

When you joined the church, you were asked, "Do you profess the Christian faith as contained in the Old and New Testaments?" You answered that question in the affirmative. In order to profess or to publicly acknowledge and claim that which is contained in the old covenant and in the new, one must become a student of the scriptures, knowing what the Bible teaches.

Paul and Timothy anticipated a time "when people will not put up with sound doctrine, but having itching ears, they will accumulate for themselves teachers to suit their own desires, and will turn away from listening to the truth and wander away to myths" (II Tim. 4:3-4). In our day, we have seen large numbers of people turning away from the truth and wandering away to myths. We are seeing a proliferation of phenomena like astrology, harmonic convergence, Ouija boards, New Age movements, and the like. The church, more than ever, needs a people who know "the sacred writings that are able to instruct you for salvation through faith in Christ Jesus" (II Tim. 3:15).

Once I stood in the quadrangle at old Oxford University in England and looked at the tower of the Bodleian Library. On that tower is the university represented in a person, and the university is kneeling to receive a copy of the King James Bible. The portrayal was exquisite to me. Oxford is one of the greatest universities the world has ever known with its accumulated wisdom going back to the Middle Ages, and still that university must kneel before the wisdom reflected in God's Book. It is a beautiful portrayal of the power and uniqueness of the Word of God. No wonder Paul said, "All scripture is inspired by God" (II Tim. 3:16a).

Why has the Bible lost a great deal of its importance and authority in our day? Dennis Campbell, dean at the Duke Divinity School, told me that there was once a time when professors in our seminaries could assume that entering theological students had a basic understanding of the scriptures. In our day, however, you can no longer assume any understanding of the Bible. Now professors begin their biblical instruction by saying, "This is Matthew, Mark, Luke, and John. These are called Gospels and there are four of them." It may be true that the Bible is the most revered, but least read, book in our culture.

Some have maintained that the Bible has lost much of its authority as a result of biblical criticism. I'm not too sure about that. Intellectual integrity requires us to approach the scriptures from the perspective of scholarship and faith. Perhaps the one thing that I would add to my own seminary training in the Bible would be an additional question. Consider the story of Jesus and the woman who had been taken in adultery. The story found in John 8 is a footnote in some translations. Our intellectual integrity makes it important for us to know that the story is contained in some of the ancient manuscripts of the Bible, but is missing in others. Therefore, some translations put it in the main text; others add it as a footnote. When I was a student, we talked about who may have written such a passage if Jesus did not. We talked about when it may have become a part of the text and asked many other important questions of the text. The one question, however, that begs to be asked is "Is it true?" If the scripture in question is true to the character of Jesus Christ, and I believe this story is, then you had better treat it as a truth. You had better read it, inwardly digest it, and seek to live according to its principles. You can wait until you get to heaven to find out for sure who wrote it.

If our study of the Bible leaves us with more doubt than faith, we are in trouble. When doubt dominates faith, you don't have to tell anyone, it becomes obvious in all that you do.

When we first moved to Houston, a church member took me out to play golf at the River Oaks Country Club. When we came to the eighth hole, I was teeing off first. The eighth hole is a par 4 with a dog leg, or a sharp turn to the left. There is a pond in front of the tee and without giving it much consideration, I hit one of my best drives and drove the ball over the pond and was left with a short pitch to the green. After I had hit my big drive, my church member friend said, "Bill, you aren't supposed to hit the ball over the pond, you'll drive the ball into the water. All of the members out here lay up and then go for the green." I've played that golf course many times since that day some seven years ago, but I have never been able to drive the ball over that pond again. I swing so hard I almost jump out of my shoes, but I simply can't get it over the water. You see, I have learned that you aren't supposed to do that. My friend planted a doubt in my mind that conquered my confidence. When one no longer believes that Jesus Christ is "the way, the truth, and the life," that Christ is ultimately important for every living person, then that attitude surfaces in one's approach to preaching, evangelism, teaching, and all the work of the church. After all, we didn't say that Jesus is "the way." He said it. That isn't our narrow claim that we hold; that's his claim that holds us. When we no longer firmly believe the scriptures, it shows itself in many devastating ways.

Christians are partially responsible for the loss of biblical authority. Many well-meaning people have abused the scriptures by making them say things they don't want to say. I think about the brochure that was widely circulated during 1988. Perhaps you received a copy. I'm sure the people who spent large sums of money printing the brochure and mailing it had every good intention. You will recall the brochure entitled "88 Reasons Why Jesus May Come Back in 1988." I was curious about a paper that claimed the ability to tell us when Jesus is returning. I sat down to read it on the day I received it. I knew that the first thing the writers would have to deal with is the scripture that declares, "But about that day and hour no one knows, neither the angels of heaven, nor the Son" (Matt. 24:36). Surely enough, that scripture was dealt with on the opening pages. The writer said that we couldn't tell the day and the hour because of all the different time zones. It's one time in Texas; it's another in New York, another time in London, and so forth. Thoughtful people who prize intellectual integrity are turned off by such reasoning. Not many appreciate someone's attempt to go "one up" on Jesus and to reveal things that even our Lord confessed he did not know. As we draw closer to the end of this century, we are going to encounter many more wild theories and predictions. We must remember that any attempt to make the scriptures say the day and the hour or the season for our Lord's return is an abuse of the scriptures.

New Christians should not begin their study of the Bible by reading those books that are most difficult to understand. The book of Revelation, for instance, loses much of its scary properties when understood. In order to understand that book, however, one must be thoroughly grounded in biblical imagery both from the Old and New Testaments.

Start your study of the Bible with one of the Gospels, an account of the life of Jesus. Learn to read the Bible both to learn its content and as a devotional exercise. Begin to acquire a good set of commentaries so that your own insights may be supplemented by those who have given a lifetime to biblical studies.

An important part of joining a fellowship of Christians is learning to study the Bible privately and in the company of others. Your own observations will be shaped, focused, and sometimes corrected by the shared insights of a company of Christians.

Many people no longer study the scriptures because they don't like what the Bible says. That was essentially the problem that Paul and Timothy confronted. They had to deal with the sophists who specialized in rationalizing almost any kind of self-serving behavior. In our own day we are seeing the truth, as we have historically understood it, abandoned in favor of modern trends or fads.

Some time ago a bishop in London made headlines by declaring that the church should abandon our historic position on sexual morality. When someone asked him how he could embrace such a position, he responded by saying that when a standard is held up for centuries and people consistently ignore it, perhaps we had better change our standards. What a tragic misunderstanding of the scriptures! The Bible clearly teaches that we are not to be conformed to the world, but to be transformed by the renewing of our minds. Indeed "the grass withers and the flower falls, but the word of the Lord endures forever" (I Pet. 1:24). Somebody has rightly said that the church that marries the spirit of this age will be a widow in the next generation. Even Omar Bradley, a military man, possessed a more accurate understanding of the scriptures than did the bishop. Bradley declared that we set our course not by the lights of every passing ship, but by the stars. We have been given "the faith that was once for all delivered to the saints" (Jude 3).

Our generation is a lot like the man who was riding his motorcycle along a south Georgia highway on a warm summer afternoon when he had an accident. The man claimed he was riding along a straight road, watching the light poles out of the corner of his eye as he drove past them. Indeed the man claimed that he was mesmerized by the poles set at equal distance along the highway. He was so taken by the light poles that when the road suddenly made a sharp turn to the left and the poles continued straight, the man followed the poles! Consequently, he injured himself and his bike rather severely. Then he sued the light company. The injured man maintained that when the road made a sharp turn to the left the poles should have followed the road. The Court did not substantiate his claim.

Many people have abandoned the scriptures because they don't like what the Bible says. They have made a sharp turn in their lives and the Bible has proved to be very unaccommodating. The Bible is, after all, "useful for teaching, for reproof, for correction, and for training in righteousness" (II Tim. 3:16). Some people don't want to be corrected or reproved.

Some see the Bible in much the same light as Alcibiades saw Socrates. Alcibiades, that spoiled man in Athens, confessed that he did not like Socrates, because every time Alcibiades saw the philosopher, Socrates made Alcibiades see himself for what he really was.

We do not have to study the Bible for long before we come to the conclusion that we aren't reading the scripture, but rather the scriptures are reading us. That is why John Wesley, who wrote many books, called himself a man of one book. The Bible is the Church's book. It is the ultimate authority by which all theologies are tested. United Methodists have a great heritage in understanding the Bible in that we read it from the perspective of reason, tradition, and experience. We agree with James Black, a great Scottish preacher who said, "If the Church puts the Bible on the shelf, the Church will not be far behind" (*Preaching*, Jan./Feb. 1989, p. 46).

Some months ago I read in the papers about the sale of a Gutenberg Bible. This particular Bible, printed in 1455, the first to be printed with movable type, was auctioned at a total cost of $5.3 million. The article called the Gutenberg Bible "the most expensive book in the world." As I read the article, I thought, if that Bible is to simply stay on a shelf and not be read, then it really isn't worth anything. If, however, someone reads and studies the Bible and as a consequence is "instructed unto salvation," made complete and equipped for every good work, then $5.3 million isn't a down payment on how much it's worth.

One November afternoon I received a telephone call at the office from my wife, who asked me if I could come home. I drove home and found my wife sitting on the living room floor with letters strewn all about her. She had been searching through the attic for Christmas decorations, getting ready for the Advent season, when she discovered an old box. In that box carefully packed away, she found all of the letters that she had ever written to me. The year before we were married my wife attended school at Wesleyan College in Macon, Georgia. I was a student at South Georgia College in Douglas, Georgia, some 120 miles south of Macon. We wrote each other every day, sometimes twice each day. There in the old box she found all of the letters that I had received from her during that year.

We sat on the floor for a long time reading those old letters. Sometimes we laughed, then again we cried, as we relived that year some thirty-four years ago. Finally, as we put away the letters and moved toward the kitchen for our evening meal, I thought, that isn't the second time I've read those letters or even the third time. I read each of those letters on the spot, just as I received them at Box #4, South Georgia College. I would read the letters again on the way to my dormitory room. After having reached my room, I would close the door and sit down for a long thoughtful reading of every line. Then the chances were quite good that the next morning I would pick up the letter and read it once more before I packed it away in my letter box. That isn't surprising, is it? That's the way it is when you're in love and you receive a letter from someone who loves you.

The Bible is God's collection of letters to you. He loves you and he wants you to read your very important letters.

8

— MEDITATION —

The Receptive Spirit

Rejoice in the Lord always; again I will say, Rejoice. Let
your gentleness be known to everyone. The Lord is
near. Do not worry about anything, but in everything
by prayer and supplication with thanksgiving let your
requests be made known to God. And the peace of
God, which surpasses all understanding, will guard
your hearts and your minds in Christ Jesus.

Finally, beloved, whatever is true, whatever is honorable, whatever is just, whatever is pure, whatever is
pleasing, whatever is commendable, if there is any
excellence and if there is anything worthy of praise,
think about these things. Keep on doing the things
that you have learned and received and heard and
seen in me, and the God of peace will be with you.
(Phil. 4:4-9)

While a divinity student at Boston University, I had
the privilege of studying under Dr. Howard
Thurman. When we came into the room where
Dr. Thurman taught his course on spiritual resources and
disciplines, there was always absolute silence. We sat there
until we overcame all of our nervous fidgeting and Dr.
Thurman finally broke the silence. Generally he said
something like this: "Now, young people, if you have gotten
still inside and are able to view the world through quiet eyes,

we will proceed with our lesson." He was calling us to a life of disciplined reflection, the same meditative life to which Paul was calling his friends at Philippi.

In the last chapter of Paul's letter to the Philippians, the eighth verse, Paul declares, "Finally, brethren." All of us who have spent some time in the church know exactly what it means when a preacher says "finally." It usually means absolutely nothing. The preacher generally has at least two or three more points. Paul is the typical preacher at this point because after he says, "Finally, brethren," he then goes on to give us a list of virtues and qualities that are most praiseworthy. After he finishes that wonderful list, he then writes a thank-you letter to his friends at Philippi, sends greetings to them, and then closes with the doxology—a benediction.

But let's give the Apostle credit. He is positive, isn't he? He concludes that list by saying, "Do this." And he begins by saying, "Think about these." He did not say "don't." He did not cast it in the negative, but in the positive. That is far better than when I first went before the Board of Ministerial Training and Qualifications. I was a frightened eighteen-year-old when I went before that board, and the only question I remember is, "Do you promise not to drink, smoke, or cuss?" That was put in the negative. It has since been taken out of the *Discipline* of The United Methodist Church because it was legalistic and negative. Frankly, I have mixed feelings about taking it out because I am afraid if we get too free some preachers might come along and feel that they ought to drink and to be good old boys and girls as a way of reviving the church. I'm glad, however, that we do not have such a negative statement in terms of ministerial qualifications.

Paul was positive. Paul knew the lower side. He knew we do not always have the elevated thoughts to which he is calling us. If you do not believe he knew the darker side, just read Romans 1. Read I Corinthians 6 and read Galatians 5. It is interesting now to see a few well-meaning, but misguided persons reading those passages and saying "Paul really did not mean what Paul said he meant." We know Paul knew what he was talking about and we know he knew something about the underside, the lower side. He chose to recommend that our thinking be in the positive mode.

In so doing, he was being faithful to his Lord, because Jesus made a powerful statement about that when he told the story about the man who swept his house free of the unclean spirit, but left it empty. When the unclean spirit came back and found the house swept and empty, he came back in and brought six more unclean spirits with him. So the last state of the man was worse than the first.

You cannot live in a vacuum. You cannot just talk about what people are supposed to refrain from doing. The only way we can rid our minds and lives of undesirable elements is to put something in their place. It is the "expulsive power of a new affection." The Apostle knew that. He did not give the Philippians a list of negatives, he gave them something positive to think about.

We know that it is difficult to think about abstract virtues—"whatever is true, whatever is honorable, whatever is just, whatever is pure, whatever is pleasing, whatever is commendable, if there is any excellence and if there is anything worthy of praise, think about these things" (Phil. 4:8). To meditate simply means to reflect upon. We reflect all of the time. It means to ponder, to let your mind dwell on it. Our minds work all of the time. If you ever ask someone "What are you thinking about?", and he or she is serious when he or she says "Nothing," call the doctor. That person has problems. It isn't that our minds do not work, but that our thoughts are upon different things and not the things of God. Our society is attuned to noise. Our society is attuned to action.

I get some of the most pathetic letters from prisoners who watch our services on television. As they try to explain why their lives have gotten into such terrible messes, invariably they will include this sentence, "I just was not thinking when I did that terrible thing." *I was not thinking*. They were not pondering; they were not seriously reflecting. It is not an easy thing to which we are called when Paul says, "Think on these things."

How can we meditate? We are exhorted to learn a foreign language by putting a tape player under our pillows while we sleep at night. I see runners going out to run beside the bayou with antennas going up out of their caps. Our noise level is awful. Did you ever have to sit at a red light beside a car in which the radio is blasting? You have your windows up as tight as you can get them, and you wonder if your poor ears can stand it. That is our kind of world. Noise—people have to have noise. People get up in the morning and turn on the television because they cannot stand a quiet house. They get in their car and automatically turn the radio on because they cannot stand the quiet. Everybody has to be hearing something, doing something. It isn't any wonder that Richard Foster, in his book *Simplicity*, said that this society is dominated by the inane concept that the only reality is action. Do something. He turns the phrase and says that we should, for God's sake and our own, stand there and not just do something.

We must remember as we think about this difficult task of Christian meditation that it is Christian. We do not just meditate for the sake of meditation. We know there are a lot of other kinds of meditation going on these days. People meditate for health reasons, and I can understand that. You are healthy if you know how to meditate effectively, because when we meditate on these things to which Paul points us, the peace of God is shed abroad in our hearts. We have an inner tranquility, and of course, our blood pressure is better and everything else is better if we have inner tranquility. Our stress level goes down if there is inner tranquility. We understand those things. Christian meditation, however, doesn't just gloss over our problems.

We do not just meditate for the sake of meditation, certainly not like the divinity cults that we see springing up all over the place. The divinity cults have as one of their primary attributes the fact that they point people to themselves. If you are looking for answers, look within yourself. If you have a problem, look within yourself to find the answer. Look deeply within yourself and you will find God. E. Stanley Jones told about a woman who said that when she first encountered that doctrine she felt as if she had wings. All of her life she had felt condemned by her sins. She had believed she was a worm, and now she felt as though she had just sprouted wings and could fly. But two years later she was flatter than a pancake. She said she found out that when you are self-centered you are a declining, decaying person (E. Stanley Jones, *In Christ* [Nashville: Abingdon, 1961], p. 123).

The God who calls us to abide in him has said it so plainly, "Because apart from me you can do nothing" (John 15:5). So we do not meditate to look for the answer within ourselves. We are guided in our meditation by Romans 12:2: "Do not be conformed to this world, but be transformed by the renewing of your minds, so that you may discern what is the will of God—what is good and acceptable and perfect." In other words, our behavior is being formed and shaped by our meditation. Our character is being shaped and molded by our meditation. And it is a discipline. It is one of those holy habits that, unless it is pursued every day, unless it becomes a part of our lives—like combing our hair and brushing our teeth—is not going to amount to very much.

It is discouraging to hear people say, "Well, I tried that a couple of times and it did not do anything for me." I think about that tourist who went over to old Oxford. He went into one of those old colleges and saw there in the quadrangle a beautiful plot of grass. All of the quadrangles have them, and each college is justifiably proud of them. If you are not a professor or some dignitary, you are not permitted even to sit on that lawn. Some tourist seeing that magnificent grass asked one of the gardeners, "How did you get grass like that?" And he replied, "Oh, it was not hard. We just watered it and mowed it and took care of it for four hundred years." It was not very hard. All it took was four hundred years. When you see someone who has inner tranquility and is someone in whom you can see the peace of God operative under all circumstances, you know it did not come instantaneously. It is the product of a lifelong habit of Christian meditation. We are talking about a discipline. We are talking about finding a time and a place every day for meditation.

The psalmist said that he would meditate when he was on his bed. I do not recommend that, especially for beginners. I am not saying you cannot reach the place in maturity when you might be able to do that someday, but I do not suggest that for us. I would recommend the morning hour for you and for me. I have not gotten to the point in my life when I can meditate on my bed, because I generally do not have any trouble going to sleep.

So, find a time and a place to read your Bible. It does not take any preparation for us to get into the Bible. Start out reading your Bible, next do your meditation, and then say your prayers. You may find an order that works better for you, but that has been the one that has worked best for me. I read my Bible, have my quiet time of meditation, and then say my prayers. It is difficult to shut out the noise and activity of the world, but the benefits are many.

When I begin to get centered on Christ inside myself, I am almost overwhelmed by a flood of things I need to do. I find it necessary, therefore, to have a notebook handy so that I might write down all of the things I remember during the first part of my quiet time. Somehow I can set all of these clamoring demands aside if I write them down. Then I can go back to the supreme purpose of my meditation, which is to receive direction and meaning for my life through God.

Howard Thurman, my teacher said, "Silence is the door to God" (*Deep Is the Hunger*, p. 18). When we refuse to be still and know, we are obscuring the part of our soul that is sensitive to God. Our traffic, our busyness, is obscuring it. Elijah did not find God in the wind or in the earthquake or in the fire, it was in the still small voice. Meditation can help you find your way back to God. If you have lost some vitality from your experience and you do not feel close to God anymore, Christian meditation can help you find your way back.

I do not know how it is with you, but every time I have gone to a large motel complex, after I have signed in, the desk clerk always turns her map around and quick as a flash, she says, "You are here." She starts pointing me to my room and invariably I have to ask her to repeat her directions. However, I have discovered one thing about maps, motels, and finding your way to any destination: You cannot get there unless you know where you are starting from. The first thing she is going to show you on that map is where you are. You are here—that is what she will say.

Christian meditation, after I read the word of God, has proven for me to be the best way to discover where I am. I read the word of God, and then in a time when there is no pretense, a time when I am trying to be totally honest, I lift up my life before the penetrating light of God's Holy Spirit and by grace determine where I am. We can hold our days, our ambitions, and our desires up until God reveals the roots of our pride, if we have the nerve to do that. When we finish seeing where we are, we are going to be so overwhelmed by the love and the grace of Jesus Christ that we are going to fall on our knees with a prayer of thanksgiving, which ought always to be a part of our prayers. You can tell when someone has been to the Great Thanksgiving because the proof of the content of our thanksgiving can be found in the humility it inspires—people who know themselves are kinder, gentler, and more loving people. Systematic meditation will help us find our way back to God. More than that, it will help us enjoy the peace of God. It will give us strength and stability in our lives.

You see, every time we meditate, we write and rewrite our history. As we write and rewrite our history, we recall those times, those moments, and those experiences when God's grace was sufficient for us—just like David, who, when he went out to face the giant Philistine, recalled the times that God had been with him in the past. It is amazing that he was doing this as a boy. No wonder he was a man after God's own heart. What was he thinking about when he went out to face this giant? Surely he was thinking about the fact that God, who delivered him from the paw of the lion and of the bear, could deliver him from this Philistine, too.

You see, when you are a person of reflection and you have accumulated a repository of faith, when the world falls apart on you, you are not going to overreact. You have a history and you are going to sit down before God to rehearse your high moments and draw on the repository of your faith. Sometimes you are going to relive the low moments, too, and will thank God for the all-sufficient nature of God's grace. It is going to help you know God's peace, and the God of peace is going to be with you. We have to be very intentional in what we think, because it is

90

true, whatever we think about all day is what we are or what we are fast becoming. The Bible says, "As he thinketh in his heart, so is he" (Prov. 23:7, KJV). If we think elevated, high, pure, and noble thoughts, we become that kind of person.

Alexander Maclaren talked about two artists who were living in whitewashed rooms. One of those artists painted beautiful pictures of the Madonna and the Risen Christ and all kinds of other lovely, uplifting pictures. The other artist painted lewd obscenities. But then Maclaren said that both of them had to live in the rooms they painted. Our thoughts fit us for our place. Our thoughts design the kind of world we live in. We go to our own place, Maclaren says, and our kind of place is determined by what we think about all day long.

Do you remember that story out of ancient mythology about Hercules and Antiochus the giant? Hercules, the mighty man who was given all the tests for his strength, came at last to grapple with Antiochus, who was a very powerful person in his own right. Hercules would get a good grip on Antiochus, only to discover that when he threw Antiochus to earth he would come back stronger than ever. Hercules would wrestle Antiochus some more, throw him to the ground, and still he would come back stronger than ever. Finally, Hercules discovered what was happening. Antiochus was drawing strength from his source, the earth. Mother Earth was the source of his strength. Then Hercules lifted Antiochus high above his head, got him away from the source of his strength, and crushed the life out of him.

The world, with all of its obscenities and all of its lewd noises, cannot crush from our lives the life of Jesus Christ unless we let it lift us from our Source. Think about these things. Let your mind dwell on them and then do them—and the God of peace will be with you.

9

— FORGIVENESS —

A Christian Response

For if you forgive others their trespasses, your heavenly Father will also forgive you.

For this reason the kingdom of heaven may be compared to a king who wished to settle accounts with his slaves. When he began the reckoning, one who owed him ten thousand talents was brought to him; and, as he could not pay, his lord ordered him to be sold, together with his wife and children and all his possessions, and payment to be made. So the slave fell on his knees before him, saying, "Have patience with me, and I will pay you everything." And out of pity for him, the lord of that slave released him and forgave him the debt. But that same slave, as he went out, came upon one of his fellow slaves who owed him a hundred denarii; and seizing him by the throat, he said, "Pay what you owe." Then his fellow slave fell down and pleaded with him, "Have patience with me, and I will pay you." But he refused; then he went and threw him into prison until he would pay the debt. When his fellow slaves saw what had happened, they were greatly distressed, and they went and reported to their lord all that had taken place. Then his lord summoned him and said to him, "You wicked slave! I forgave you all that debt because you pleaded with me. Should you not have had mercy on your fellow slave, as I had mercy on you?" And in anger, his lord handed him over to be tortured until he would pay his entire debt.

So my heavenly Father will also do to every one of you,
if you do not forgive your brother or sister from your
heart. (Matt. 6:14; 18:23-35)

John and Charles Wesley and General James Oglethorpe, with whom the Wesleys traveled to the colony
of Georgia in 1735–1736, became good friends during
their long voyage. One day the men were chatting, and the
subject of forgiveness came up. General Oglethorpe was
adamant that he made it a practice never to forgive. John
Wesley responded, "Well, sir, I hope you never sin." Wesley
knew that our forgiveness has always been tied to our
willingness to be forgiving.

The Lord's Prayer has been called the model prayer, or
the pattern after which the disciples of Jesus are taught to
pray. It is revealing when one studies the prayer closely to
recognize that after Jesus had given it to his disciples, he
chose the petition having to do with "forgive us our debts as
we forgive our debtors" to explain and to expand. Jesus'
direction to enlarge on the teaching on forgiveness means
that Christians must pay close attention to the petition that
our Lord especially wished to emphasize. More than that, in
the sequence of the prayer, he put it just after the request
for daily bread. Putting it as he did right after *daily,* we
believe Jesus intended that the practice of forgiveness
should be a daily exercise, one of those continuing holy
habits that marks the life of a Christian disciple.

The emphasis on forgiveness was so important, as a
matter of fact, that Jesus lifted it up in the Sermon on the
Mount when he declared, "Blessed are the merciful, for
they will receive mercy" (Matt. 5:7). Then he emphasized it
again in his prayer, expanded on it, and gave us one of his

most memorable parables on the same theme in the eighteenth chapter of Matthew. In that parable, you will recall, he told about the king who settled accounts with his servants. They brought forth one servant who owed the king the enormous sum of ten thousand talents, or ten million dollars. Why, the whole gross national product of Galilee, their richest province, was only three hundred talents, or three hundred thousand dollars! We are talking about a sum of money more than the gross national product of three provinces put together. It was an unheard of amount of money.

When the servant came before the king, obviously unable to pay the debt and knowing that the legal code at that time permitted him and his family to be sold in order to pay the debt, he fell on his knees and said, "Lord, have patience with me and I will pay you." That was surely a wishful thought, but he begged for mercy nevertheless. He must have been happily astonished when the king freely forgave him all of that huge debt.

As the parable continues, the forgiven servant went out into the street and met one of his fellows who owed him twenty dollars. He himself had just been forgiven ten million dollars. Now he met someone who owed him twenty dollars. Those hands that have been wringing in agony earlier when he was before the king suddenly went around the throat of that fellow servant, and he began to choke him, saying, "Pay what you owe." It was almost as if the servant he was choking had been an eavesdropper. He used the same speech his assailant had used before the king, saying, "Have patience with me and I will pay you." But the man refused, and the second servant was thrown into jail.

Now there were people there who saw the transaction, and they ran to tell the king. When the king heard about it, he sent for the servant whom he had forgiven and said, "You wicked servant, I forgave you all of that debt and now you would not forgive your brother even a paltry sum. You are going off to jail until you pay the last penny." In other words, Jesus is saying, "How can you, who have been forgiven so very much, now refuse to forgive your brothers and sisters for their smaller sins against you?"

The matter of forgiveness has always been central, hasn't it? Reinhold Niebuhr said that forgiveness is the central issue in Christian theology. He said that the church has been slow in becoming aware of it, but it is crucial. Having been a pastor for a number of years, I readily agree with Niebuhr. The problem of forgiveness is a central problem among God's people.

Clarence Jordan has given us a kind of historical summary of this matter of forgiveness. He said that a long time ago people practiced unlimited retaliation—you injure my child and I will wipe out your entire tribe. You take one of my cows and I will burn your house down and kill your children. Unlimited retaliation was practiced among primitive peoples. He then went on to say that when we received the Law of Moses, which taught us that we should practice an eye for an eye and a tooth for a tooth, we learned limited retaliation. Although that may sound severe, it represented a great step forward in the progress of our understanding of religion. The punishment had to fit the crime. No more than that, an eye for an eye and a tooth for a tooth.

Then he goes on to explain that there was a time when we practiced limited forgiveness. We would love our neighbor and hate our enemy. We would forgive those people whom we loved. Jesus talked about people like that. He said that you do good to those who do good to you, you love those who love you, and you give good gifts to those who give gifts to you—but even the sinners do that. That is limited forgiveness. Then when we come to Jesus' teaching in all of its fullness, we have unlimited forgiveness. "But I say to you, love your enemies and pray for those who persecute you" (Matt. 5:44). That is unlimited forgiveness and a great challenge, isn't it?

Many of us are still challenged on the level of in-house forgiveness—struggling with forgiving those people who are going to have a chance, if they will wait a few days, to forgive us for something we have done. We have a hard time forgiving the people with whom we live, the people who we love. We keep score: "I have forgiven you ten times and you have only forgiven me nine." We go to all kinds of ridiculous lengths. We forget that to live with someone is to practice forgiveness on a daily basis. We have a hard time with one another, like the man about whom I read who was seen running frantically upstream beside the river. Someone stopped him and asked, "Where are you going in such a hurry?" He said, "My wife fell into the river and I am trying to rescue her." The friend said, "Then why are you running upstream? You ought to be searching downstream." The husband replied, "You do not know how contrary my wife is."

We have a hard time with a contrary husband or a contrary wife. We get hung up on in-house forgiveness, and all the while the real challenge for mature disciples is out there with those persons who deliberately hurt us. We sometimes experience hurt in a cruel, imperfect world—there are people who, as Joseph said about his brothers, "meant it to be evil." We are not talking about an accidental happening that we can easily overlook.

It's like some of the letters I received after the Houston Declaration came out (a theological declaration emphasizing the primacy of scripture). I think some of the writers really meant what they said to me. I would stay awake sometimes thinking about those letters. One particular person made all kinds of hurtful comments. Among other things, he said, "You preachers in the big churches, most of you were born with silver spoons in your mouths." I immediately wrote that brother back and said, "I know that I was born and reared in Snipesville, Georgia (population: approx. twenty-five), thirteen miles from the nearest paved road. I accept the fact that I am one of the privileged few. I graduated from Snipesville Academy and I know I have been blessed." What do you do when someone deliberately says something or does something to bring hurt?

I was preaching once in a multi-state gathering. During the course of the days I was speaking there, I had the joy of preaching to a retired missionary. He had spent his entire life on the mission field and had even lost his wife there. He had spent his life in sacrificial service thousands of miles away from home. It was such a joy to preach to him and to interact with him after the service. His clothes, his person, indicated that he had not had an easy time. Back in the days when he was on the mission field it was especially harsh. When he smiled, it was an imperfect smile because there had been no dentistry available where he had been serving. His entire person spoke of what he had suffered. On the last night of that meeting, I was shocked when he came to tell me about an experience that had occurred years earlier, when someone had done a terrible thing to him. As he spoke to me about that experience, his wonderful face became twisted in a new kind of agony. He said, "I have never forgiven him for what he did." I wanted to take him into my arms and rush to the altar. Here was a man whom we all admired, and yet he was carrying a horrible resentment in his soul that had been eating away at him for years. I thought, "My God, if a man like that puts his soul in danger because of an unforgiven sin against him, how much more am I in peril?" All of us, when someone does us harm, have our very souls put in jeopardy. We cannot do what that man did without grave damage to our inner selves. We cannot bank our resentments and just hold on to them through the years. We have been given a standard by our God. He laid down his life for us in the person of Jesus Christ. Christ died praying, "Father, forgive them; for they do not do not know what they are doing" (Luke 23:34). That standard will forever be the guide for us in our relationships with others.

Look at the parable to which we referred earlier. The king did not get angry with the servant because he owed him ten million dollars. He did not get angry with him about the size of the debt. When does the word *angry* appear? The word *angry* appears when the forgiven servant refused to forgive his brother. Then the king was angry—not about the debt, but about the harsh, unforgiving attitude. The forgiveness the servant had earlier received was rescinded, his debt was once again placed around his neck, and he bore it to the jail. God canceled the canceled debt. God took the debt that he had taken away earlier and put it back onto the one who had shown in his own life that he refused to mirror the mercy of God. God's love had not found a corresponding echo in that man's soul. That man expected God to do for him what he was unwilling to do for others, and God gave him his debt back. It is scary, isn't it? No wonder Jesus wanted to explain it further. We are forgiven as we forgive—"forgive us our debts as [in direct relation to] we also have forgiven our debtors" (Matt. 6:12).

God has taken the initiative, however. God has forgiven us first and he has offered us the grace and the spirit to enable us to be forgiving persons. Why is it so hard for us to forgive? Maybe we have forgotten the magnitude of our own sin. That does happen; we do forget. If we are aware of how much God has loved us, then it makes us more loving and tolerant toward other people. Jesus asked Simon the Pharisee which man would love a creditor most. "Simon answered, 'I suppose the one for whom he canceled the greatest debt.' And Jesus said to him, 'You have judged rightly' " (Luke 7:43).

I heard a bishop say that modern people are offended if preachers suggest that we are all sinners. Many of today's people think about a sinner as being a drug dealer or someone who engages in a heinous crime. "They are sinners, and I am a respectable citizen; I have never been in danger of going to jail." We forget that the Bible has different words for "sin." One of them means missing the mark. We do not come up to everything God is expecting of us. We simply miss the mark. Another is that we step across the line. We have not always been completely honest. We have not always told the whole truth. Another one is that we slip across the line. We are good for the most part, but now and again we lose control. Another one has it that we simply rebel; we say, "I do not want anybody telling me what to do." Another is the word *debt,* which was used in the Lord's Prayer, and really means duty. Have you always done your perfect duty toward God and toward the rest of humankind? If you have, I would like to meet you. I have never met anyone who has done all of those things. Sometimes we forget the magnitude of our sins. Our sins put Jesus Christ on the cross, and he died saying, "Father, forgive them; for they do not know what they are doing."

Sometimes we simply do not want to forget the grievances we have toward others. We reinforce and continue to reinfect all of our old wounds. Many times I have heard people say, "It is all right now; I have forgiven him, but let me tell you what he did to me." As they start to relate the deed, they become animated, their eyes shine, they start to make gestures, and suddenly all of the dreadful old fires are burning again. Like a flame that has almost gone out, their resentment is down to a spark or two, and then they punch it alive, and it flames up once more. They just will not let it go. They keep pulling the scabs off the old hurts. They will not let themselves heal.

A preacher reminded me of this unfortunate tendency to hold on to our hurts, as I was telling him about a man who had hurt me deeply when I first decided to go into the ministry. The man had told me that I would never make it as a preacher because of my background. My friend listened to me, and he had apparently heard me tell the story before. He looked me steadily in the eye and said, "Don't you think you are ready to let that go? Aren't you about ready to turn loose of that?"

A Moravian missionary went to the Eskimos and could not find a word for forgiveness in their language. So he put a compound word together that meant "no longer being able to think about it anymore." I like that definition. I like that old folk wisdom that says, "You can feed a puppy and starve a lion, and if you do it long enough, the puppy will finally whip the lion." Some things we just need to starve to death. We can starve our grudges and resentments until, by God's grace, they disappear. You see, when we have been forgiven, we also accept Christ into our lives, and through his Spirit, he calls us to be imitators of himself. He offers us the grace that not only covers our sins, but also enables us to forgive the sins of people who do wrong things to us. That kind of grace received and offered can change your home, can change your life, and can change your world.

I had the opportunity to see the play *Les Miserables* in London. What a marvelous adaptation of Victor Hugo's novel! The play was all about social injustices and the part poverty plays in crime, but to me it was also a moving expression of grace. Jean Valjean, the principal character, had been put into prison for nineteen years for stealing a loaf of bread in order to feed his sister's family. Finally, he is set free. A bishop is the only one who befriends the embittered man. Valjean rewards the bishop by stealing some of his silver. He is caught red-handed by the police, having stolen from the only man who has been kind to him. The bishop is called in to press charges, but instead of pressing charges, he gives Jean Valjean a pair of silver candlesticks as well. Jean Valjean is never the same after that. He demonstrates grace to an orphan child and raises her as his own. He prays a beautiful prayer for the young man who later marries the girl whom he has reared as his own daughter. He even forgives and frees the policeman who wants to put him back into prison. To everyone he touches he offers grace. In the last scene of the play, as he is singing his death song and is about to leave this world, in front of him on the table, holding two burning candles, are the candlesticks—a reminder of the bishop who had first offered mercy to him.

Every time we enter the sanctuary, we have the symbol of our forgiveness before us—the cross of Jesus Christ. Accept the grace offered to you daily and extend it to others in the name of Jesus.

10

— EXEMPLARY LIVING —

Guarding the Faith

But as for you, man of God shun all this; pursue righteousness, godliness, faith, love, endurance, gentleness. Fight the good fight of the faith; take hold of the eternal life, to which you were called and for which you made the good confession in the presence of many witnesses. In the presence of God, who gives life to all things, and of Christ Jesus, who in his testimony before Pontius Pilate made the good confession, I charge you to keep the commandment without spot or blame until the manifestation of our Lord Jesus Christ, which he will bring about at the right time—he who is the blessed and only Sovereign, the King of kings and Lord of lords. It is he alone who has immortality and dwells in unapproachable light, whom no one has ever seen or can see; to him be honor and eternal dominion. Amen.

As for those who in the present age are rich, command them not to be haughty, or to set their hopes on the uncertainty of riches, but rather on God who richly provides us with everything for our enjoyment. They are to do good, to be rich in good works, generous, and ready to share, thus storing up for themselves the treasure of a good foundation for the future, so that they may take hold of the life that really is life.

Timothy, guard what has been entrusted to you.
(I Tim. 6:11-20*a*)

Have you ever had the experience of paying a rather large entrance fee to spend the day in an amusement park? More than likely, at the time you paid the fee the attendant used a special stamp to put a mark on the back of your hand. The mark is largely invisible, but if at any time during the day you left the amusement park for a time and then chose to reenter, all you had to do was pass your hand beneath a special light and the mark indicating that your admission had been paid would be in clear view. That mark would, of course, enable you to regain admission to the park.

As a baptized Christian, you now bear the mark of Jesus Christ in your life and person. An unbelievable price has been paid for you by Christ on the cross. Now you can understand the solemn exhortation that the apostle Paul gave to his spiritual son when he exhorted Timothy to "guard what has been entrusted to you" (I Tim. 6:20a). You have also received a great legacy in your baptism and in the resulting responsibility that you have taken before the altar of the church when you promised "according to the grace given you to live a Christian life." More than that, you promised to keep God's will and commandments and to "walk in the same all the days of your life." Our promise to live an exemplary life is the same promise and challenge that the apostle Paul was exacting from Timothy.

As a beginning minister, I preached lots of youth revivals. One of the books I most enjoyed using was entitled *Salty Christians*. I not only liked what that book had to say, but also I loved the title—*Salty Christians*. We are called to be the salt of the earth, to be someone who makes a difference in the world, a salty Christian. How is it that Christians in our day are often perceived as passive people who really do not make much impact on our culture or upon our world?

Oliver Wendell Holmes once said that he had thought seriously about going into the ministry until he began to see that many of the ministers whom he knew looked and acted like morticians. I think that was a bad rap for the morticians. Some of my best friends are morticians, and they are sensitive and caring people with a special ministry. What Holmes was saying was not complimentary either to the morticians or to the ministers.

I remember my oldest brother coming to see me right after I had gone into the ministry. I was serving a student appointment at the time and he, still trying to come to terms with the fact that I had gone into the ministry, heard about a man in the community, an alcoholic whose problem was out of control, who was giving me a hard time. The man was engaging in all kinds of harassing activities like blowing his truck horn in the middle of the night as he sat parked in front of my parsonage.

When my brother came to see me, he said, "Well, why haven't you taken care of this matter?" I said, "I am trying to." He said, "What do you meant you are trying to? Aren't you man enough to whip him?" I replied, "Charles, I just don't deal with people that way anymore. That is a part of my old life and I am trying a new technique these days." "Well, if you cannot handle him, tell me where he lives because I can handle him for you," Charles retorted. "No, I am not going to tell you where he lives," I replied. Charles's parting shot went something like this: "When you gave Jesus your heart, did you give him your guts as well?"

Many times Christians come across as having lost their courage. We appear to surrender our intestinal fortitude and our ability to make a difference. We come across as a timid people. Paul says we are a people who are doing battle, who are fighting the fight of faith. We are people who make a difference. Because we do make a difference using Christian means, we must be prepared for criticism.

Once I received a telephone call from a person who was complaining about our efforts in trying to deal with the drug problem in Houston. He wanted stiffer penalties for all offenders and blamed us "do-gooders" for part of the problem. As I listened to the complaints, I thought about that old evangelist who, when someone was telling him all the things they did not like about the way he did evangelism, responded by saying, "I like the way I do evangelism a lot better than the way you don't do it."

We live in a strange world and we are called to make a difference, but if we try to make a difference, we are going to be heavily criticized. The moment we try to give leadership to any program, the world is going to attempt to shoot us down.

It's not just the drug problem, either. The same kind of thing happened when some of us took some initiatives with the problem of the homeless in Houston. It happens any time you try to make a difference. The only way you cannot be criticized is to do nothing. And there are a few people who will criticize you for that, too.

I remember one of the stories about Mayor LaGuardia that I heard from a guide while on a Gray Line tour in New York City. One night in 1935 in the depths of the depression, Mayor LaGuardia went down to preside on the Municipal Bench as he was qualified to do. Someone was brought before him who was advanced in years, a grandmother probably, or maybe a great-grandmother, who was accused of stealing a loaf of bread. She was being prosecuted; she had been caught in the act of stealing the bread to feed her family. Mayor LaGuardia asked the accuser if he were going to press charges, and the man said, "Yes, I am. I live in a rough section of town and if I let her get away with it, they would empty my shop. I have to press charges." With that, Mayor LaGuardia said to the woman, "You have broken the law and you have to pay the price for breaking the law; the fine is ten dollars." Then, knowing the woman did not have the money, LaGuardia took ten dollars from his pocket and gave it to her. Then he said, "Now I am fining everyone in this court room fifty cents. Bailiff, take up the fines." He took fifty cents from every person in the courtroom and that came to $47.50. Mayor LaGuardia gave it to the woman also, and then he addressed the spectators: "I am fining you for living in a city where a grandmother has to steal to feed her grandchildren."

In the same spirit, we must say to every one of those well-meaning persons who criticize our efforts, as long as the Church is in the world and as long as God gives us power to respond, wherever there are people who are hurting, wherever there are people in pain, wherever there are people who are oppressed, then our Church must be in the middle of it. We must be underneath the suffering with the everlasting arms of Christ trying to help human beings live as children of God. Hudson Taylor, the great missionary, said that if you have become a Christian, your family ought to know it, your neighbors ought to know it, the persons with whom you work ought to know it; it ought to make a difference in everything you do. Even your cat and dog ought to be happy that you are a Christian. We are called to live an exemplary life.

Paul did not just leave Timothy with a nebulous exhortation. He said, "I want you to set your sights on something; I want you to aim at something." Then he gave Timothy that litany of virtues. And, oh how powerful they are! Paul said, "I want you to aim at righteousness; I want you to do your perfect duty toward God and man. I want you to aim toward godliness." Do you know what godliness is? Godliness is living all of life in the awareness of the presence of God. We are all pledged to godliness.

Then he said he wants us to aim toward steadfastness. You may think that is a passive virtue, that it is just folding your hands and acquiescing, saying, "I will accept whatever happens to me." That is not what it means. It means victorious endurance. It points to a grace that enables us to triumph over the things that happen to us—the same kind of grace recently exhibited by one of our church members in Houston. She is under thirty years of age, has only been married seven years, and has two little children. She was taken to the hospital not long ago because one morning she awakened and was unable to walk. Rather quickly the impulses between her brain and spinal cord were interrupted, and now she is paralyzed. She has been to rehabilitation so that they could teach her how to handle her wheelchair and how to go about her responsibilities as a mother. She called me recently and said, "I need to talk for just a moment. I know it is going to be all right. But I was overwhelmed this evening as I was sitting here looking at my husband and children, remembering how it used to be. I just need to talk for a few minutes."

My friend is a living example of steadfastness, a steadfastness that does not require that faith explain everything, that faith provide all of the answers, but a steadfastness that enables us to claim the gift of confidence and courage that enables us to go on, even when we do not understand. That is the steadfastness to which we have been called.

Combined with the other virtues, Paul was placing quite a load on that young man Timothy. How in the world could Timothy carry that load? How can we carry that load and live exemplary lives before a world that is pretty much pagan in its attitude? Paul gave some suggestions. He told Timothy to remember the confession that Christ made, to remember the good confession of all of the witnesses there when he made his confession, and to remember the high moments and hold on to them. They would be a source of inspiration to him.

Jesus stood before Pontius Pilate and accepted and acknowledged his own Kingship. Jesus said he was there to witness to the truth. Christ gave the good confession even when it cost him his life. We need to think about all of those witnesses who were there when we were baptized. Like Timothy, we gave the good confession in the presence of many witnesses. It ought to be a special moment when you became a Christian. It ought to be a Glory Hallelujah kind of moment, one you will never forget, when you made your confession.

When our Lord was hard-pressed and discouraged, and people were leaving him on every hand, he went back to the Jordan where John had first baptized. Why did he go back there? He could have gone because that is where he was baptized. That is where the sky opened and the Spirit descended on him like a dove. That is where he heard God's voice saying, "You are my Son, the Beloved, with you I am well pleased" (Mark 1:11). That was a high moment in Christ's life, and Paul is reminding Timothy of those holy moments when he stood before the company of witnesses and made his own confession of faith in Jesus Christ.

He also tells Timothy to remember his family. The gospel came to Timothy at considerable cost. After all, he was all that Lois and Eunice had. The Bible tells us a lot about Timothy's father by what it does not say. It simply says, "But his father was a Greek" (Acts 16:1). That was short for saying, in contrast to Lois and Eunice, his grandmother and his mother, his father was not devout, not inclined toward the Christian faith.

It is tough for a single parent. It is tough for someone to have sole responsibility for the scriptural upbringing of a child. Yet that was the plight of Lois and Eunice. Paul came to his town when Timothy was only a youth and Timothy would have known how they stoned Paul that day. He would have seen that bloody and battered apostle in whom the drive was undiminished, who got up when they thought he was dead and went back into the city and preached the gospel again. From that day on, Timothy belonged to Paul. Oh, Paul did not come back to get him until he was probably nineteen or twenty years of age, but he came back. Lois and Eunice packed his bag not knowing if they would ever see him again. He was the apple of their eye. He was everything they had, but they let him go without a whimper. "Timothy, remember, the gospel has come to you at great cost."

Some of us received the gospel at great cost from courageous people. I remember a youth minister who fought a battle with cancer and lost. Before he died, he listened to my story as I shared it with him. I had had an experience with Christ and I was determined to walk away from it; I didn't want to be a minister, I wanted to be an attorney. One night I told the young man who was a summer worker at our church my story, and I will never forget his response because it is one of the hinges on which my life turned. After he heard my story he paused for a long moment, then said, "I would think a long time before I walked away from that." Just that. But, for me, that youth worker is in the company of witnesses.

Paul is exhorting Timothy to remember all of the important people in his life and to remember that ours is a farsighted faith. I charge you to keep the commandment unstained, unspotted by the world until the appearing of Jesus Christ. Jesus Christ is coming again. He is coming for me, and he is coming for you. Finally, he will come for the whole world. One by one we are going to face Christ. That is a great source of encouragement.

I remember a story Pierce Harris told thirty years ago when he was the pastor of First Church, Atlanta, Georgia. We used to go downtown from seminary to hear him preach. Harris said that he had some stewards in his church who were so mean that he was not even going to tell them about hell—he was going to let them be surprised. Now that is really being mean, isn't it? I do not know how we can be so casual about a morally indifferent life. We have gotten the idea in our culture that immortality is everybody's due—that we are all going to live forever, no matter how we lived on earth. When someone dies, no matter the circumstances, people say, "Well, they have peace at last" or "They are going to a better place." But Paul says, "He alone . . . possesses immortality" (I Tim. 6:16). If we do not through faith in Jesus Christ lay hold on eternal life, it is none of ours. Paul is saying to Timothy, and to us, that we are the trustees of the faith. This generation passes away and another generation is coming—but we are the link between the generations; we are the trustees of the faith.

I drove a new car into a car wash not long ago. The attendant who was wiping it dry said, "This is a beautiful car!" I replied, "Yes, it is, but it is not mine." Then he asked, "What is yours?" I said, "Nothing." I could have added, "As for mortals, their days are like grass; they flourish like a flower of the field; for the wind passes over it, and it is gone" (Ps. 103:15-16). I am only a trustee, but I have responsibility for some things during my time here on earth.

That is the insight Paul had for Timothy and for all of us. You are a trustee. Guard the deposit that has been made in you. You have been given a treasure; you are a custodian of the faith because of the promises that you have made. Someday the present is going to change to the past, and as you fight the good fight, remember the testimony of Paul: "I have fought the good fight, I have finished the race, I have kept the faith. From now on, there is reserved for me the crown of righteousness, which the Lord, the righteous judge, will give me on that day, and not only to me but also to all who have longed for his appearing" (II Tim. 4:7-8). What could be more encouraging than that?

I was expecting the early morning call from her doctor. I knew she was very ill, and I had promised to be there with her at the end. I dressed hurriedly, and as I drove to the nursing home, I reflected on all of the service that the tiny eighty-five-pound woman had given to her church and community. Long after she had to stop visiting the lonely, taking food to the hungry, and giving comfort to the grieving in person, she continued to send cards and to write letters. She literally gave herself to others until the last days of her life.

Now, my unselfish friend had summoned her pastor because it was to be her last day on earth. I called my office and told them I would not be coming in that day. I pulled a chair close to her bed and took her thin, tired hand in mine. All she wanted, she said, was for me to hold her hand until her son, who lived in a distant city, could get there. Several hours later her son arrived. He sat on the other side of the bed and held her other hand. Shortly after noon the Son of God came and took my precious friend home.

As I left the nursing home and headed for my car in the parking lot, I thought, "Holding the hand of someone who needs you until the Son comes is not a bad way to spend a morning. In fact, it's the best way to spend a life!"

Guard the faith. Guard it through your exemplary living and caring. Aim at righteousness, godliness, and steadfastness, and one day when the Son comes, you will receive a crown.